"In *The Imagination Machine*, Martin Reeves and Jack Fuller take us on a jolly jaunt from cave paintings to AI-generated images, from the Princes of Serendip to the worldview of the *Umwelt*, from LEGO to Play-Doh and the founding ideas of Amazon and Disney. Prepare to be inspired."

—**BOB GOODSON**, President, NetBase Quid

"In an age when corporations are getting ever larger, business models are evolving faster, and artificial intelligence is changing the way we work, companies need imagination more than ever. Rather than treating imagination as an unruly art, Reeves and Fuller convincingly show how companies can systematically cultivate and harness it."

—**GARY HAMEL**, coauthor, *Humanocracy*; Visiting Professor, London Business School

"*The Imagination Machine* explains how the power of imagination can be kindled and harnessed. It's a must-read for every corporate leader or employee."

—**STEVE BLANK**, entrepreneur; Adjunct Professor, Stanford University; and coauthor, *The Startup Owner's Manual*

"Before you can build the Next Big Thing, someone has to come up with the idea on which it is based. In this charming but thorough exploration of the role of imagination in business and society, Martin Reeves and Jack Fuller take us on a tour of what imagination is, why it's so essential, and how you can cultivate it. A tonic for these highly uncertain times!"

—**RITA McGRATH**, author, *Seeing Around Corners*; Professor, Columbia Business School

"A truly inspiring and beautiful book. It not only explains how renewal from within is the key to sustaining long-term business success; it also gives business leaders the hands-on tools and methods to go about it."

—**GEORG KELL**, Chairman, Arabesque; founder, United Nations Global Compact

"*The Imagination Machine* is insightful and timely. As the pandemic has altered many work habits for good, and when the boundaries between management and leadership blur, imagination indeed becomes an increasingly necessary corporate resource."

—**MARCO ALVERÀ**, CEO, Snam

"Martin Reeves has done it again. With Jack Fuller, he maps the future for business leaders with *The Imagination Machine*—an incredibly practical and thought-provoking read on stoking imagination within corporations. In order for our companies to flourish in this post-Covid era, it would behoove us to act on these powerful concepts without delay."

—**JIM LOREE**, CEO, Stanley Black & Decker

"*The Imagination Machine* is a fascinating and practical guide on how to harness imagination to develop and implement transformational ideas, which are so needed in these fast-changing times."

—**SUSAN HAKKARAINEN**, Chairman and CEO, Lutron Electronics

"*The Imagination Machine* belongs in the library of any leader who is serious about developing an industry-leading innovation capacity."

—**JOHN HALEY**, CEO, Willis Towers Watson

"In the era of the Internet of Everything, competition between enterprises will become a competition to fuel the imagination of employees. Therefore, only by believing in human value maximization and turning employees from tools of implementation into autonomous entrepreneurs can we win. *The Imagination Machine*, which puts forward some powerful questions and propositions, is well worth reading."

—**ZHANG RUIMIN**, Chairman and CEO, Haier Group

"To create innovative solutions, organizations need both a mechanism that triggers employees' imaginations and a system that transforms the ideas employees produce into practical, applicable projects. This book is a good reminder of the importance of fostering creativity in the workplace."

—**MASUMI MINEGISHI**, Chairperson and former CEO, Recruit Holdings

"In an age of VUCA, especially in light of the coronavirus pandemic, it is challenging for organizations in any sector, including NGOs, to innovate and keep innovation alive. Drawing on multidisciplinary insights, this book argues that imagination is upstream of innovation and articulates a six-step methodology for managing and stimulating imagination, providing a powerful set of tools to enable organizations to get the "imagination machine" up and running."

—**XU YONGGUANG**, Founder, Project HOPE, China; Honorary President, Narada Foundation

— THE —

IMAGINATION
MACHINE

How to Spark New Ideas and Create Your Company's Future

THE
IMAGINATION
MACHINE

**MARTIN
REEVES**

**JACK
FULLER**

HARVARD BUSINESS REVIEW PRESS • BOSTON, MASSACHUSETTS

Library of Congress Cataloging-in-Publication Data
Names: Reeves, Martin, author. | Fuller, Jack, 1985- author.
Title: The imagination machine : how to spark new ideas and create your company's future / Martin Reeves and Jack Fuller.
Description: Boston, Massachusetts : Harvard Business Review Press, [2021] | Includes index.
Identifiers: LCCN 2020047906 (print) | LCCN 2020047907 (ebook) | ISBN 9781647820862 (paperback) | ISBN 9781647820879 (ebook)
Subjects: LCSH: Imagination. | Creative ability in business. | Success in business.
Classification: LCC BF411 .R44 2021 (print) | LCC BF411 (ebook) | DDC 153.3/5—dc23
LC record available at https://lccn.loc.gov/2020047906
LC ebook record available at https://lccn.loc.gov/2020047907

ISBN: 978-1-64782-086-2
eISBN: 978-1-64782-087-9

Contents

Dramatis Personae

Charles Merrill & Winthrop Smith .... American bankers who reimagine banks like supermarkets

Shelby Clark & Andre Haddad .... Who imagine, start, and run Turo

Ole Kirk Kristiansen, his son Godtfred &
Jørgen Vig Knudstorp .... Founders of LEGO, and its chairman

Prof. Susan Blackmore .... Psychologist who writes *The Meme Machine*

Omar Selim .... Who reinvents quantitative ESG
His children .... Who surprise Omar

Profs. Judea Pearl and Karl Friston .... Who teach us how the brain works

Risto Siilasmaa .... New board member who saves Nokia

巻口 隆憲 *(Takanori Makiguchi)* .... Who leads an entrepreneurship institute within Recruit Holdings

山口文洋 *(Fumihiro Yamaguchi)* .... Who imagines StudySapuri

Dr. Bill Janeway .... Venture capitalist who reads nineteenth-century English novels for inspiration

Jane South .... Artist and Chair of Fine Arts, Pratt Institute

Thomas Aquinas .... Philosopher who is charitable to opposing mental models

Dr. Mikael Dolsten .... Swedish-American chess player, head of research at Pfizer

张瑞敏 (Zhang Ruimin) .... Leader of Haier, who kicks off imagination by smashing a refrigerator

Prof. Eduard Marbach .... Phenomenologist living in Swiss mountains

Walter Anderson & Billy Ingram .... Who invent the idea of a chain restaurant

Blaise Agüera y Arcas .... Explorer of machine imagination and art at Google

Nitin Paranjpe .... Who sends an entire company (15,000 people) to the field

Johann Georg Hamann, Denis Diderot &
Jean-Jacques Rousseau .... Villains who spread confusing ideas about imagination

Tim O'Reilly .... Silicon Valley's public intellectual who popularizes Web 2.0

Susan Hakkarainen .... Chairman and CEO of Lutron, who puts herself in the customer's shoes

Prof. Simon Levin .... Leading US mathematical biologist and eclectic thinker

Generative Pretrained Transformer 3 (GPT-3) .... Charismatic, although unconscious, AI

Philip Clouts .... Jazz musician, son of poet Sydney Clouts

And other CEOs, entrepreneurs, scientists, philosophers, &c.

— THE —

IMAGINATION MACHINE

Chapter One

INTRODUCTION

Corporations have changed the world radically in so many areas: medicine, consumer goods, transport, finance, agriculture, entertainment, communications. And they've done so by combining organizational abilities with the unique human capacity to imagine: the ability to see and create things that had never existed.

Who in the 1500s would have thought it would be possible to manufacture so many shoes and distribute them around the world? Who would have thought that writing and staging plays would turn into the television and movie industries, with performers given the same status as the nobility in ancient Rome? Who would have thought that a few people and a team of machines could run farms the size of small countries? If we had never imagined, we would have never taken the steps that led us to these once unimagined realities.

Imagination is needed now more than ever. Since competitive advantage is increasingly short-lived, driven by rapid evolution of the technological and business environment, companies constantly risk stagnation. Since the 1960s, the average number of companies exiting the *Fortune* 500 has increased by 36 percent annually, and the proportion of industries in which the top player has led for more than five years has nearly halved. Outperformance more quickly fades to the mean (see figure 1-1).[1]

Companies also face declining market growth, driven by maturing demographics. Since 1970, worldwide GDP growth

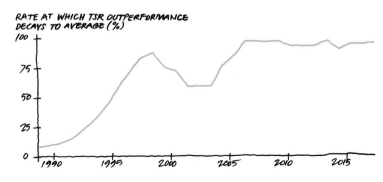

Figure 1-1 Outperformance more quickly fades to the mean

Source: Data from S&P Capital IQ; BCG Henderson Institute analysis.

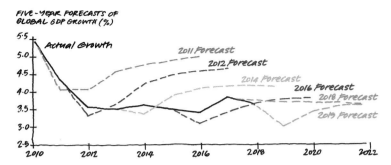

Figure 1-2 Global growth projections have shifted downward

These projections are from the fall IMF outlooks of each year; 2020 projections are not shown due to impact from Covid-19. *Source:* "A Bad Time to Be Average," by Hans-Paul Bürkner, Martin Reeves, Hen Lotan, and Kevin Whitaker, July 22, 2019. Used by permission of the BCG Henderson Institute, a division of Boston Consulting Group. All rights reserved.

Who would ever have imagined that one day suits of armor would be affordable for all!

has fallen from 5.5 percent to 3.3 percent, and over the last decade, expectations have consistently fallen (see figure 1-2).

When everything is growing, it's harder to see the need to imagine, explore, and experiment. Companies float on a rising tide. People have more money to buy more of your product, or an increasing population means there are more people who buy. But if you are in Europe, for instance, which grew at 5.5 percent in the 1970s and is growing at 2 percent today, you need good ideas. Participation in aggregate growth becomes harder, so growth has to be created through imagination.

And this has to happen at a higher frequency than ever. Companies need to reinvent themselves and their offerings again and again. A great model for making money and meeting people's needs may quickly become unexceptional or even a liability, as yesterday's assets and procedures become a source of inertia.

Corporations today all started as scrappy, entrepreneurial efforts, guided by imagination. Retaining or recovering this capacity in today's ever larger corporations is the basis for their ongoing vitality and success.

At the same time, the world is facing a range of complex, collective problems:

- Epidemics

- Climate change

- Inequality

- Populism and social polarization

- Lack of fresh water

- Mental health issues

- Cognitive overload

- And so on

No business can afford to operate as though it is a world unto itself, independent of the systems of society and nature it is embedded in. As we have seen in the Covid-19 crisis, things seemingly far removed from a business's concerns can suddenly undermine its ability to function. The problems listed above impact all humanity and our institutions. To address them, we will need to draw on our capacity for imagination. And business can play a central role in this.

As a side note, it is interesting to reflect that imagination itself is partly responsible for our troubles. Yuval Noah Harari, historian and author of *Sapiens*, points out that since the beginning of agriculture, humans have been solving

Who knew, 15,000 years ago, how much trouble the imagination would cause?
Source: Courtesy of Philippe Psaila.

problems with their imagination, but that reimagining often merely sets the stage for new problems.[2] We figured out how to cultivate wheat and invented ways to store it, but then wheat attracted scavengers and rivals, so we invented walls and defenses, but then settlements fostered infectious disease . . . and so on.

Any imaginative solutions will surely lead to further unexpected problems. But there is not much we can do about this, other than notice the species-level irony and make the next wave of imagination a productive one, sharpening our approach to harnessing this unique power.

Finally, although artificial intelligence (AI) is still developing, its transformational power is clear. Unlike previous waves of technology, AI threatens to replace not routine physical work but routine cognitive work, much of which we call "management." This raises the question: What will the humans do? The answer is that we will be left with the skills that are still unique to humans. Competitive advantage will accrue to firms that can shift focus to these skills, that develop ways of working to get the most out of human imagination and higher-level cognition, while lower-level analysis and decision making are increasingly automated.

Like the revolutions that followed from steam, steel, electricity, and the combustion engine, we won't get the full benefits of the technology unless we reorganize our ways of working. When we invented the electric motor, we didn't get the benefit until we reorganized the factory.[3] Because AI is a cognitive technology, we won't get the benefits unless we rethink the *cognitive* aspect of business—unless we build

It's the only job we haven't been able to turn over to AI—plugging them in.

We often think of business as about managing the externals, but what is going on in the brains of people here? *Source:* Jetstar Airways (jetstar.com).

companies that cultivate and harness the most valuable mental capacities of the humans within them, working together with intelligent algorithms.

Beyond the assessment of people's skills around hiring, promotion, and a handful of other tasks, the cognitive dimension of work has not been a big focus for business. Historically, the process of industrial production could afford to not care much about what was going on inside people's heads, because it required little more than compliance with prescribed roles. It's a focus that has continued to the present. Compared to, say, the industry of psychotherapy or great sports teams, people in business are primarily concerned with externals, comparatively less with the potentialities and nuances of the human mind.

Yet the rise of AI will likely shift the focus of human work to higher-order capacities. Businesses will need to be-

come much more knowledgeable about and competent at extracting value from unique processes in human brains. To draw an analogy, modern business applies a huge amount of ambition and competence to formidably difficult tasks, like extracting oil from miles under the ocean or from organic matter embedded in rock. We will need to apply that same level of seriousness—the desire to do it a hundred times more effectively than anyone has before—to the task of nurturing and drawing from imagination in human brains. In the early days of oil, people would just dig around and occasionally strike oil. That's roughly where we are at with imagination today.

In addition to changing how we work within businesses, AI also opens possibilities for radical new services and busi-

The early days of extracting oil. This is our current level of sophistication around extracting imaginative ideas. *Source:* George Rinhart/Corbis Historical via Getty Images.

I don't know which one— he just said follow a star . . .

meet collective and individual needs, companies must tap into the full humanity of the people who work for them— the reward of which is sustained growth.

• • •

ness models that will transform industries and fulfill unmet needs. With the rise of AI, we will rethink how we generate energy, build infrastructure, defend countries, manage and enhance health, educate ourselves across a lifetime, save and invest, communicate, gain self-knowledge, and get entertained. Firms that cultivate and use imagination effectively will be pioneers in these spaces of possibility, finding revolutionary new offerings and the growth they unlock.

For the sake of restoring the vitality of our companies, and for the societies these companies serve, we must better harness imagination. To imagine and realize new ways to

This book is about how to harness the unique human faculty of imagination. We have written it primarily for business leaders who wish to revive and capture the imaginative powers of their organizations. We are motivated by frustration at the declining creative capacities of mature companies and the aspiration that we can not only rehumanize our overly financialized and proceduralized corporations but put the human capacity for imagination at the center of collective enterprise.

Though we have a long way to go in understanding imagination, we do have important insights about it from cognitive science and the humanities. The aim of this book is to draw on the best knowledge we have about imagination and filter this through practitioners' minds—our own experience and interviews with business leaders—to produce a practitioners' guide to building and operating an imagination machine: a company that systematically harnesses imagination to drive growth.

We use the word "machine" because imagination is a tool, and companies are tools to serve human ends. Though imagination is somewhat unruly, there is no reason we cannot develop a more systematic approach to cultivating and using it, just as business has done in other domains that depend on quirky characteristics of the mind, like advertising or human resources. And although the word "machine" may evoke images of factories from the last century, modern machines are increasingly flexible and intelligent. A company worthy of the name imagination machine is one that can consistently reinvent itself and what it offers to the world.

This book is about the mind, but not only the mind. Harnessing imagination entails dealing with the mind, action, and their interaction. It is not only about individual creativity, but how minds can interact, creating collective imagination and momentum to turn ideas into new realities. And it is not only about product innovation; it is a book for business leaders who want to re-envision their entire enterprise and increase its imaginative potential. We will look at the complete life cycle of ideas from inspiration to new realities. We will look at how businesses can be transformed to capture imagination. And we will explore how AI might be incorporated into an organization so it can become even more productively imaginative.

Our journey begins by understanding what this familiar but ill-defined capacity is all about. What is imagination? How does it work, and how can it be put to work? We explore this in the next chapter.

Chapter Two

WHAT IS IMAGINATION?

In order to harness imagination, we first need to understand what it is: to define it and what it can do for us, and to understand how it works.

The Power of Imagination

We can most clearly see what imagination is by comparing humans and other animals. An animal like a cow or a fish lives in the realm of what is. A goldfish works with just what is in front of it; it has no standpoint to reflect on its situation.[1] It can't create a mental model of a different, better kind of fish tank more aligned with its aspirations to flourish as a goldfish.

Humans, in contrast, can explore the realm of what is not. A hunter-gatherer could create a mental model of a better kind of basket or what the hunt might be like the following day. In business, we can consider what a company might be like if it were restructured or new products or services we could invent. This capacity to mentally explore the not-yet-existent allows us to deliberately create new things and shape the world around us.

We define imagination as "the ability to create a mental model of something that doesn't exist yet." This is also known as "counterfactual thinking": the ability to create mental objects that are not merely representations of the outside world.*

In business, we spend much of our time in the realm of what is. We think factually, looking at data or a particular

---

* "Creativity" comes from "create." It's a general word meaning the ability to bring something into being. "Innovation" is likewise a general word, meaning creating something novel. "Imagination," in contrast, refers to a specific mental process occurring in human brains: putting together mental models of things that don't exist yet. Imagination—the mental activity within and between brains—is the essential human element of the programs of innovation and creativity in companies. But imagination also extends beyond programs of innovation: it is not just used for inventing new products and services, but for fundamentally rethinking the mental model on which a company is based, even rethinking an entire industry or envisaging new industries.

*Sakkanakki Babili—Warriors have been attacking
the HR department in the outer provinces!*

An increase in productivity this week, sir . . .

situation, trying to determine what is going on. This makes sense. Managing a business involves keeping a complicated effort going; many large businesses are bigger than most cities have been throughout human history. Walmart, for example, with its 2.2 million employees, is ten times the size of the great city of ancient Babylon. It makes sense that most of the time our minds are taken up with just keeping the machine running.

There are times, though, when we need to explore what is not, but could be. In crises like Covid-19, for example, we tend to be consumed with the question "What is happening to us?"—the factual question—to the exclusion of the imagination-provoking, counterfactual question "How can we create new options?"

When we think counterfactually, we put aside mental models we habitually rely on and create new ones. Haier, for example, now the largest appliance manufacturer in the world, transformed itself in the 1980s. At the time, the company was in crisis: the factory was run down and in debt. The new chairman, Zhang Ruimin, decided the company would have to move beyond making passable but lackluster refrigerators. He pulled seventy-six fridges off the production line—any that had even minor faults—and asked employees to smash them up.[2] It was a symbolic act to shift thinking from the factual to the counterfactual: What could we do if we got rid of the existing system? *Without* imagination, all you would be doing is destroying the current reality.

The Evolution of Imagination

How did imagination evolve? It appears to have developed as a tool to solve novel problems: How should we respond to this fire at the edge of our camp? How can we best cooperate in this terrain to hunt this animal? Or how might this person's erratic friend react if I treat them in this way?

One evolutionary precursor to imagination seems to be the capacity to name or classify situations. Chimpanzees have this skill: they can learn abstract symbols for situations and point to them when they want an additional banana or the room heated up.[a] What chimpanzees are not particularly good at, however, is rearranging symbols to make novel combinations. A chimp will likely not rearrange symbols to ask if the banana can be heated up. In contrast, human children instinctively apply new concepts to everything. Once a child discovers the idea of cooking, they might ask if grapes can be cooked, if juice can be cooked, if books can be cooked, and so on. If they learn about sadness, they might ask if the dog is sad or if the clock is sad, or observe that the sun might be sad in the evening.

In the evolution of imagination, one crucial development was the ability to divide the world up more discretely and then manipulate how those parts relate. Humans can isolate the concept of heating up and apply it to many things, beyond one fixed idea of heating up the room. As evolutionary biologists Eva Jablonka and Marion Lamb note, this flexibility shows in our language, which "gives the unit, the word, great freedom to move from context to context . . . no longer constrained by referring to one particular situation."[b]

This ability to analyze and isolate concepts has allowed humans to take ideas from one domain and apply them analogously to another, creating mental models of never-before-seen situations and perhaps from there, mental models of not-yet-existent things and situations.[c] This has led to new concepts, tools, modes of social organization, and territorial expansion.

No, silly! Mountains can't heat up!

How imagination evolved is still a much-discussed topic in science. But we might draw one tentative conclusion: that the analytical capacities underpinning and enhanced by language—the ability to observe, divide up the world conceptually, and create new relations between parts—enable imagination. Dissection and conceptual clarity might be prerequisites to, rather than the antithesis of, imaginative thinking. Analysis supports synthesis. Rearranging the parts to create new wholes is easier when we have a deep understanding of the parts.

NOTES

a. Eva Jablonka and Marion J. Lamb, *Evolution in Four Dimensions: Genetic, Epigenetic, Behavioral, and Symbolic Variation in the History of Life* (Life and Mind: Philosophical Issues in Biology and Psychology) (Cambridge, MA: MIT Press, 2005).

b. Jablonka and Lamb, *Evolution in Four Dimensions*.

c. Clive Gamble, *Settling the Earth: The Archaeology of Deep Human History* (New York: Cambridge University Press, 2013).

A cow, for instance, could not understand the point of bull-dozing a moderately useful barn, whereas this might prompt an imaginative human to start making a mental model of something that doesn't exist yet.

Grounded Imagination

Imagination is not just random thoughts unhinged from reality. Rather, it rests on a causal understanding of reality (see the sidebar "Humans versus AI"). To the extent we understand the dynamics of this world—*why* things are the way they are—we can play with recombining and changing things in ways that still make sense and are feasible.

We can compare imagination to other functions of the brain that are more or less tied to reality (see figure 2-1). As far away from imagination as it is possible to be is a state of mere being. This is the life of a plant. A plant has no self-awareness and is guided by its immediate environment. It has no brain to be able to release itself from the present.

With a human brain, functional possibilities open up beyond a plantlike state. There is conscious perception, a self-aware mode of operating that is tied to the outside world. Perception is constrained by what is out there—which is useful if we want to get an accurate picture of the world. Opposite perception is dreaming, an un–self-aware operation of the brain that is not constrained by the outside world; rather, we spend time in our inner world of scenarios, memories, and symbols while we sleep.

In between perception and dreaming is imagination, a self-aware mode of thought that is somewhat constrained.

Figure 2-1 Imagination versus dreaming and perception

Imagination *loosens* the correlation to reality; we are playing with possibilities, rather than trying to get a precise picture of our environment. But it doesn't cut the tie to reality. Effective imagination works with the laws of nature and other knowledge we have about the dynamics of the world—insights about human nature, practical wisdom gained from running a business, or lessons from history, for example. In imagining, we alter some parts of reality while remaining grounded in what we know about the rest of reality.

We might daydream of a flying giraffe or an interplanetary pipe to take the Earth's oceans to Mars, but these are absurd, because they are outside the way the world works. Imagination, in contrast, draws on the depth of our factual models to inform and ground our counterfactual models. For example, in business, we could ask the counterfactual question: "What could an office supplies company be?" and imagine some radical and fascinating answers, drawing on our mental models of other industries, history, psychology, and technology.

. . .

What can imagination do for us? We can see this in figure 2-2. The two boxes on the left cover the factual realm, divided into what is inevitable and what is incidental. Inevitable things are features of the world like gravity, uncertainty, or permanent aspects of human nature. Incidental things are changeable, like laws, having cars in cities, patterns of customer demand, how profit is measured, the role of HR, and so on.

The two boxes on the right cover the counterfactual world, divided into impossible things, such as hyper-light-speed travel, a mind-reading machine, or pet dinosaurs (though some things that seem truly impossible turn out to be possible), and imaginable possibilities. This upper-right box of possibility is the one that is interesting for business.

Imagination allows us to explore the space of what is possible—the counterfactual realm—like a mining expedition to uncharted territory. It allows us to explore, and it

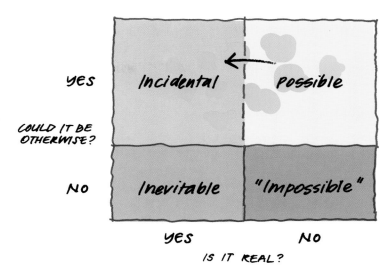

Figure 2-2 **Exploring and mining the space of what is possible**

allows us to bring things back: early-stage counterfactual ideas that may eventually transform the business. Becoming skillful at *harnessing* imagination means becoming skillful at doing this collectively within a company: exploring and moving things from the unreal to the real.

How Does Imagination Work?

To harness imagination in business, we need to dissect this capacity to see how it works, not only at the level of the individual, but in the context of a company: how it works between as well as within minds and how imagination is intertwined with action. Let's look at the life cycle of an idea, from an inspired thought to creation of a new reality.

Humans versus AI

Computers can't do counterfactual thinking, at least for now. To see why, we can compare the cognition of humans versus AI. As described by computer scientist and philosopher Judea Pearl, almost all current AI relies on a basic form of cognition: noticing correlations.[a] A computer can notice that fire and smoke occur together, for example, or that Amazon customers who liked *Rambo: Last Blood* also liked *Fast & Furious 7*.

But humans can think at a level above merely noticing correlations. We can understand causes. We can say *why* phenomena are linked: why fire causes smoke; why customers who liked *Rambo* liked *Fast & Furious*. Understanding causes means that we don't just notice that things in the world occur together; we grasp the underlying dynamics that produce the relationships. Drawing on psychology, we could guess that people liked *Rambo* and *Fast & Furious* because they are looking for heroic stories, perhaps because they feel they lack this in their lives. An AI could only tell you these two movies will likely occur together in online purchases.

Because the human mind is full of rich models of the world that capture causal relationships, we can think at one level higher again: imagination, or counterfactual thinking. When we think counterfactually, we draw on our causal understanding of the world, but we alter some parts and their relationships. As psychologists Caren Walker and Alison Gopnik describe it:

> Conventional wisdom suggests that knowledge and imagination, science and fantasy, are deeply different from one another—even opposites. However, new ideas about children's causal reasoning suggest that exactly the same abilities that allow children to learn so much about the world, reason so powerfully about it, and act to change it, also allow them to imagine alternative worlds that may never exist at all . . . It is because we know something about how events are causally related that we are able to imagine altering those relationships and creating new ones.[b]

To illustrate all three levels of cognition: an AI could identify a correlation (level one), for example, that people buying coffee are 60 percent likely to also buy a bagel. But this doesn't tell you about causality (level two): Are most people coming for the coffee and buying bagels as an extra? Or is it the other way around? Once you know the causal relationship, you can

The Seduction

One prominent theory about how the brain works, the Bayesian theory, holds that our brains update themselves based on surprising new inputs. A surprise is the beginning of imagination: an event that leads our minds away from familiar ways of thinking.

We can see surprise at the level of a neuron. The definition of surprise is, "a difference that makes a difference."[3] When a cell gets no surprising input, it has nothing to report. If it met up with other neurons for a chat, it would be the boring one,

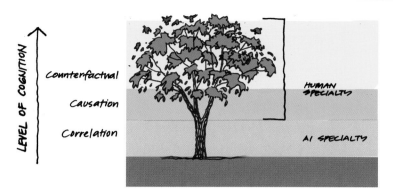

Levels of cognition from correlational to counterfactual thinking. *Source:* Adapted from Judea Pearl and Dana MacKenzie, *The Book of Why: The New Science of Cause and Effect* (New York: Basic Books, 2018).

model of a new coffee loyalty program. Or you could imagine the future of food and drink. At the World's Fair in 1893, American suffragette Mary Elizabeth Lease imagined that by 1993, humans would eat only synthetic food, freeing women from the kitchen.[c] Although this scenario wasn't actually realized, it is an example of the scope of human imagination. Computers can't create this kind of somewhat-plausible scenario because they lack causal models of the world. There is no data to crunch on things that do not yet exist. AI today has no causal models to mess around with to probe the realm of possibility.

NOTES

a. Judea Pearl and Dana Mackenzie, *The Book of Why* (New York: Basic Books, 2018).

b. Caren Walker and Alison Gopnik, "Causality and Imagination," *The Development of Imagination*, ed. M. Taylor (New York: Oxford University Press, 2013).

c. Matt Novak, "Meal-in-a-Pill: A Staple of Science Fiction," BBC, November 18, 2014, https://www.bbc.com/future/article/20120221-food-pills-a-staple-of-sci-fi.

then make an educated guess about a counterfactual question (level three): What would happen if you stopped selling bagels?

Going further into counterfactual territory, you could use your casual understanding of the world to create a mental

describing its day as "same old, same old." Another neuron might have encountered something unusual and would say to the others, "Actually, I had something strange happen to me today; let me tell you." It has encountered some difference, or anomaly, and this difference has *made* a difference by affecting the entity (a neuron) that encountered it—which

goes on to make a difference in other entities (other neurons and through communication, other brains).

If your brain never encountered anything that was different from its existing mental models, it would never have cause to change its thinking. Contact with surprise—encountering something that doesn't fit—is the starting point

. . . *Mmm* . . .

for imagination. We look at how to increase exposure and receptivity to surprise in business in chapter 3.

The Idea

After encountering a surprise, the brain has a number of possible actions available to it. Neuroscientist Karl Friston has distinguished five (see figure 2-3).[4] The first of these is to *rethink*, that is, to change, recombine, and play with models in our mind to generate new ideas.* In chapter 4 we will dive into how to do this effectively.

---

* The terms "idea" and "concept" can be used interchangeably with "mental model," as in, "our idea for a new business is . . . ," or "our concept of a media company is . . ." We will use them interchangeably throughout this book. The term "mental model" is useful because it emphasizes that the mental entity is made up of components that can be removed, altered, and recombined.

A great example of rethinking in business is the development of the LEGO Group. Early in the last century, the business was a carpentry firm that had expanded into making wooden toys such as yo-yos. Then an inspiring encounter—a surprise—kicked off a transformational rethink. As told to us by the executive chairman of LEGO Brand Group and former CEO, Jørgen Vig Knudstorp:

> The founder, Ole Kirk Kristiansen, traveled to a trade fair in 1946, and encountered an injection molding machine—precision plastic injection molding was a new thing and had taken off during World War Two. Seeing this machine completely changed his thinking about what was possible. He thought, "Wow, this is fascinating. What could be done with this new plastic molding process? What could our business be like if we reoriented everything around this machine?"[5]

The Collision

Once an idea or mental model starts to develop in our mind, what can we do with it? The brain has a number of options to bring the mental model into contact with the world.

We can *refocus*, shifting our attentional filters based on our emerging idea, leading to further surprises and further rethinking. We can *move* in the world: colliding our evolving model with different geographical or social contexts. And we can *probe* the world, trying out something that provokes a re-

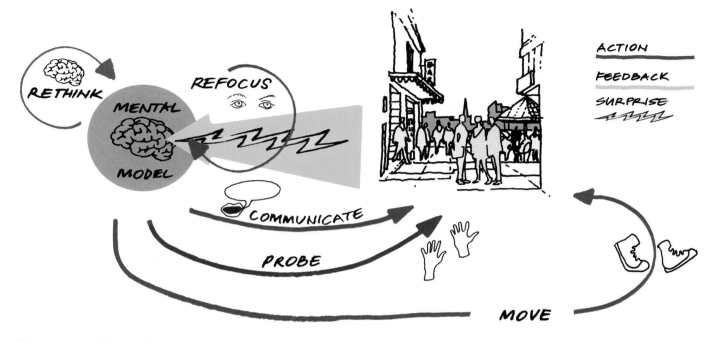

Figure 2-3 Individual actions triggered by surprise

sponse that feeds into our developing counterfactual model. During the reimagination of the LEGO Group:

> The founder actually spent an entire year's profit from the company to acquire a plastic injection molding machine, just so he could try it out—so he could play with it. Plastic toys were held in low regard, but he started producing teddy bears, airplanes, small trees, cars, small toys out of plastic. Inspired by the tractors that arrived with the aid from the US Marshall Plan, he created the Massey Ferguson tractor set with plastic parts. He really let his imagination lead him—into new kinds of products, but also, into a reconceptualization of what the company could be.[6]

By colliding our evolving idea with the world, we can use the collision to enrich our imagination. The mental model develops as the idea passes from mind to world, and back.

We will explore how to support and enhance this process in chapter 5.

The Epidemic

The other action open to the human brain, following the disruption of a mental model by surprise, is to *communicate*. Unlike other animals, we can make ideas spread: an idea can jump from brain to brain, joining imaginations together across a business, accelerating both the development and adoption of an idea (see figure 2-4).

This diagram shows the multiple-brain version of the diagram seen in figure 2-3: communication links minds as the idea spreads across multiple brains. When we communicate a still-evolving imaginative idea, we aim to *become* the surprise—the disruptive or inspirational input to other people's minds—triggering others' imaginations. When this

Figure 2-4 Imagination across multiple brains

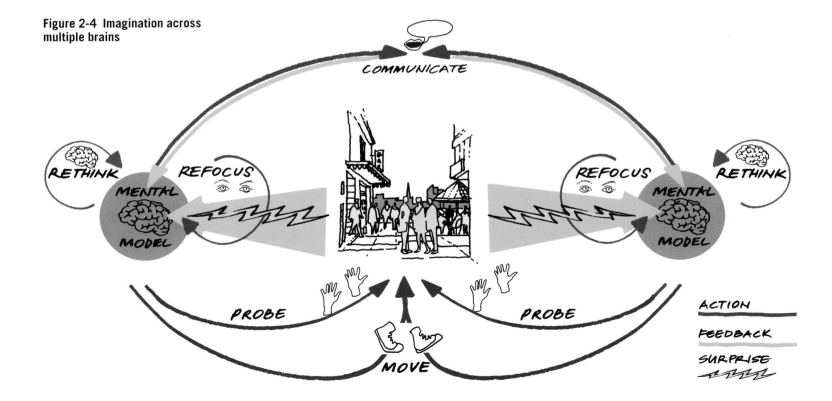

happens, it creates collective imagination, amplifying the idea by making it socially significant, and accelerating its evolution by involving others in its testing, development, and adoption. We will look at how organizations can facilitate this in chapter 6.

Collective imagination played a crucial role in developing a mental model that was core to the LEGO business. As told by Knudstorp:

> The founder's son, Godtfred, became involved in the business. At one point on a boat trip he had a pivotal conversation with a toy buyer from Copenhagen. The buyer talked about the idea of a *system* of toys where each new toy built on previous ones. They discussed this and Godtfred took the idea back to his father and others. Over some weeks they developed the idea into a kind of mental framework for the company that they shared with every employee, called the LEGO System in Play.[7]

This is a great example of ideas evolving socially. The mental model was spread in one conversation, developed through further discussion, and eventually disseminated to all LEGO's employees, sending the business in a new direction.

The New Ordinary

Developing and spreading new mental models would be pointless if it did not lead to a new reality. The goal is for an idea that began with a surprise to eventually become unsurprising: an ordinary and accepted part of reality.

Key to this is the art of codification, or writing a script so that the new thing can be realized and replicated by people far removed from its pioneers. We look at tools for doing this in chapter 7. In the case of the LEGO product, a key requirement was to bring customers into the world created by the toymakers. Indeed, the LEGO Group has become expert at writing scripts that induct people into the LEGO world. From our interview with Knudstorp:

> It's a universal, globally accessible language; because the product is designed so intuitively, everybody understands how to play with LEGO bricks. The other thing though, which is actually crucial, is creating the text-free building instructions. What's really surprising is that the building instructions are super hard to copy. Of course you can make a photocopy, but it's a big competitive advantage to be able to make great build instructions. We have a large team with very deep expertise of understanding of minds at the age of seven or at the age of fifty—what they need to know, to know how to take part in the LEGO world.

The Encore

In moving a model from the counterfactual to the factual, we create new policies, procedures, and specialized roles. Yet

Misconceptions about Imagination

A number of popular misconceptions get in the way of understanding what imagination is and how it works. It's worth noting these to avoid being misled by them.

Some of the most common myths around imagination are:

- **That it is exclusively mental**—overlooking the interactions with the world that prompt and ground useful imaginative thinking

- **That it is exclusively individual**—believing it's all down to one heroic individual, forgetting collective imagination, and that ideas that don't spread aren't useful

- **That it is unworldly**—seeing imagination as dreaming, rather than as counterfactual thinking that depends on an analytic understanding of the world

- **That it is momentary**—believing or hoping that imagination happens in a flash, rather than via deliberate mental construction and repeated collisions with the world

- **That it is mystical**—believing it can't be systematically managed, unlike other unpredictable aspects of human nature that business manages to harness

Most of these ideas can be traced to a cultural shift in Europe in the 1700s, the Romantic movement. Many intellectuals of that time were focused on rethinking what it meant to be an artist. The prevalent view was the Classical approach developed from Aristotle through scholasticism and the Renaissance: that being an artist was about learning a skill, clarifying a purpose or ideal, and building on and refining an inherited art—a systematic, collective practice—to pursue that end.[a] An example of this classical philosophy was the construction of cathedrals: extended, collective, creative efforts motivated by an ideal, for which no individual contributor took credit.[b]

In place of this, many influential thinkers, such as Johann Georg Hamann, Denis Diderot, and Jean-Jacques Rousseau

working within these dampens our capacity for surprise. As they grow, businesses face the challenge of being ambidextrous: on the one hand, having the corporate machinery to exploit developed ideas; on the other hand, being able to continually explore new ideas—to harness imagination repeatedly. A business that can do both well can be called an "imagination machine": a company able to reliably harness imagination to discover new paths to growth, transforming itself and growing over time. This challenge will be explored in chapter 8.

• • •

Imagination itself is the ability to create mental models of things that don't exist. Harnessing imagination in business,

Yes, just the three sons—a soldier, a priest, and a tragic genius.

advocated a new Romantic view: that chosen individuals—geniuses—have a mystical, mental link with a higher power, which leads them to great, iconoclastic ideas in some impossible-to-understand way. As historian Isaiah Berlin summarized: "[The Romantics] attributed freedom, self-determination, spontaneity, creative power to a transcendent self, outside the empirical universe with which men came into relationship only in comparatively rare moments in a mystical rising above their earthly selves."[c]

In this book, we seek to dispel the Romantic myths of imagination, aiming instead, in the footsteps of Aristotle, to articulate the elements of a systematic, collective practice we can rely on to foster and harness imagination.

NOTES

a. Jack Fuller, "An Investigation of the Discussion of Civilization" (thesis, Oxford University, 2012).

b. Paul Spencer Wood, "The Opposition to Neo-Classicism in England between 1660 and 1700," *PMLA* 43, no. 1 (1928): 182–197.

c. Isaiah Berlin, "Three Turning-Points in Political Thought," *Isaiah Berlin Virtual Library*, n.d., http://berlin.wolf.ox.ac.uk/lists/nachlass/romanticism.pdf.

however, requires looking at all these areas, from the individual to the collective level. The following chapters will lay out actions, principles, policies, tools, and exercises for business leaders to shape themselves and their companies to draw on imagination consistently and successfully. In addition to this handbook, you can visit www.theimaginationmachine.org for further interviews, articles, supplementary resources, and an online version of the organizational diagnostic we offer at the end of each chapter.

We begin, in the next chapter, by looking at how we can increase our exposure and receptivity to inspiring surprises.

Chapter Three

THE SEDUCTION

Every imaginative effort begins with a mental spark. Financial pioneer Omar Selim's spark came from an unexpected source: his teenage children. Selim, who was Barclays head of global markets for institutional clients for the European time zone, was preparing for a trip the following day to Johannesburg. At dinner, he and his children talked about work and life, what matters and what doesn't. "Okay, so you're going to fly there tomorrow, stay in a five-star hotel, give a speech, which probably nobody really cares about," they said. "And this is the path you've chosen to dedicate your life to?"

As Selim told us, this blunt challenge from his children actually triggered his imagination. It threw everything into question. And this trigger coincided with a situation at work that gave him a lot of time to think. Barclays had sold its investment management arm to BlackRock, with a noncompete agreement, which meant that Selim and his team, who remained at Barclays, "were not allowed to do any asset management." Selim read and thought deeply about sustainability and how finance might be transformed by nonfinancial data and machine learning. Catalyzed by the conversation with his children, he rethought the institution he wanted to work for, putting together a mental model of a new kind of asset management business. Eventually, he negotiated with Barclays to buy out existing operations and used this to set up Arabesque, the world's first asset management firm driven by AI analysis and environmental, social, and governance metrics.[1]

• • •

For imagination to be harnessed in business, it first needs to be triggered or inspired. Something needs to seduce us (*se-ducere*, to lead away) out of our routine way of looking at things into the realm of counterfactual thinking. This chapter will examine how surprise triggers imagination, actions we can take support this, and blocks to avoid. It will also describe some imagination-provoking games to play to enhance your capability, good questions to ask, and an organizational diagnostic for your business.

What Inspires Imagination?

Small surprises happen all the time, like receiving an unexpected email. But the surprises relevant to imagination are the ones that seduce us away from routine thinking and lead us to rethink deeply and inventively. These are the anomalous, challenging, unfamiliar, even incomprehensible encounters that inspire imagination.

Three types of surprise can inspire imagination: accidents—events or consequences incidental or irrelevant to what we are trying to achieve; anomalies—parts of a situation, story, or dataset that are out of the ordinary; and analogies—parallels we see between concepts or experiences, which suggest new possibilities.

For surprises to impact us, however, our minds need to be prepared. Plenty of things pass us by, but we need to *notice* them (the cognitive aspect) and we need to *care* (the emotional aspect) to spark imagination. If Selim had not cared about reforming finance, he wouldn't have started

Yes . . . but do you really *care*?

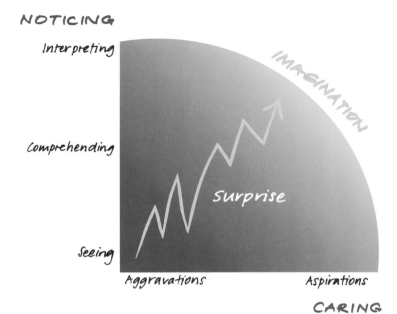

NOTICING

Interpreting

Comprehending

Seeing

Aggravations   Aspirations

IMAGINATION

Surprise

CARING

Figure 3-1 Noticing and caring to encounter the surprises that draw us into counterfactual thinking

Arabesque. Equally, if he had not noticed how machine learning was impacting other businesses, he would not have had a stock of mental models to draw on in rethinking how an asset management company could work.

The more we commit to caring and noticing, the more we create the mental context for encountering imagination-provoking surprise (see figure 3-1).

There are two ways of caring: aggravations and aspirations. *Aggravations* or frustrations drive us to change or escape from something. *Aspirations* drive us to bring something

we want or believe into being. These are important because our brains do not simply register any and all sense impressions. As neuroscientist Walter Freeman described, "the pattern generated by the cortex is not a 'representation' of the stimulus but . . . constitutes the *significance* and *value* of the stimulus for the animal."[2] What impacts us is what matters to us. Aggravations and aspirations motivate and enable us to notice.

We can notice things more or less deeply: seeing, comprehending, and interpreting. Each of these is associated with a pathology of *not* noticing, which we might recognize from business or our own lives: forms of obliviousness.[3]

Seeing is taking in new information. If we don't do this, we won't encounter any kind of surprise. If we're stuck doing only routine things every day, not having interesting conversations and not exposing ourselves to new social or geographical environments, we are stuck in "informational oblivion."

Error

Comprehending is processing something we see to understand it. We might be exposed to new information, but unless we say, "Wait, that is an interesting anomaly. Let's think about that" or "Why do you think we got that accidental result? Isn't that curious?" then we are not using our brains. If we don't put in the time or effort to process what we see, we are in "computational oblivion."

Interpreting is connecting—noticing the ramifications of one piece of information for others. Think of the difference between you and a trained biologist walking through a forest. Where you see simply a leaf, they notice the early appearance of a rare tree at an unusual elevation, implying a changing climate, which has implications for the forest as a whole. Their biological worldview allows them to interpret more: to make more  connections. If we can't draw on a rich conceptual inner world, made of deep and varied worldviews, we are in "conceptual oblivion."

When we care and notice, we get inspired more; we encounter surprises—accidents, anomalies, and analogies—that prompt us to reimagine.

Johnny! If you don't learn, you will be consigned to conceptual oblivion!!

$3 + 6 =$

How to Foster Inspiration

To harness imagination in business, one thing we must do is increase the frequency of productive surprise. We start where imagination starts, with a single brain: what actions can help you, as an individual, to more frequently use your imagination. As the book progresses, we move to the social level and actions you can take to reshape your company.

Seeing

MAKE TIME FOR REFLECTION

The most basic need is to make *time* for noticing. Given the amount of pressure on them, business leaders need to work hard to protect time for reflection.[4]

Inspiration for imagination often comes when we are reflecting: relaxing, with no pressure from urgent tasks. Archimedes of Syracuse was one of the most imaginative minds in history: he invented the block-and-tackle pulley system, the first odometer, a gigantic mirror-based weapon to focus the sun's rays on incoming Roman ships, and the formula πr^2. But he had his most famous idea while lying in a bath. Presumably relaxing after a long day, he thought about how water rises after you put something in, and if you measure that rise exactly, you can work out the volume of the object. After this realization, he allegedly ran down the street naked shouting, "Eureka!" (in Greek: εὕρηκα, *heúrēka*: "I have found it!").

It may be no accident that people often get inspired in the bath or the shower, because these tend to dampen our fight-or-flight nervous system in favor of the rest-and-digest system (see the sidebar "The Parasympathetic Nervous System"). Omar Selim told us that inspiration often happens for him in this context: "I'm sure that it's a purely individual thing. But I get most of my ideas when showering in the mornings. That's why the shower is a really good place, or a steam room in a hotel, or whatever, but I feel inspired when the temperature around me is right. I just relax. I'm not bothered with anything."[5]

In the early days of Merrill Lynch, founder Charles Merrill wrote to his business partner Winthrop Smith about the importance of taking time to reflect: "You and George Hyslop [a partner in the firm], and when I am there, me, too, should never be so busy that we cannot set aside at least one hour each day to quiet, thoughtful study and discussion of the basic principles, as contrasted with current operations."[6]

For business leaders, especially during crises, it is easy to lose the already slim time that often exists for reflection. Imagination, however, requires blocks of time with low external demands. Warren Buffett famously schedules time for a haircut in his diary, which is actually time for him to sit in a room and reflect. We need time to think about our aspirations and aggravations and to see, comprehend, and interpret, following our curiosity rather than a deadline.

Like switching on airplane mode on our phones, we need a mental switch for ourselves for "rest mode," disabling fight-or-flight functions, creating space for imagination. Some ways to do this include:

- Taking a few deep in-breaths and longer out-breaths[7]
- Taking time over a meal to rest, mentally digest, and reflect
- Listening to or playing music
- Going for a walk without your phone

PAY ATTENTION TO FRUSTRATIONS

To encounter more surprise, another action you can take is to focus on your frustrations. Aggravations or frustrations, if they don't emotionally overwhelm us, can help us care about what we notice. In 2008, MBA student Shelby Clark was cycling to a Zipcar he had rented. As he told us, "I ended up reserving the closest car to me, 2.5 miles away. And I got stuck in a snowstorm. I was biking through the snow for 2.5 miles to get to the closest car, just grumbling the whole way, when there are these cars that are covered in snow, thinking: 'Why am I passing all these cars, to get to a car? Why can't I get in *that* car? Wait . . . why *can't* I get in that car?'"[8]

This was the imagination-triggering event for Clark. He noticed and cared about (was aggravated by) something other people would have just cycled past. A row of unused, parked cars would not surprise most of us. But driven by his frustration, it stood out for him, prompting him to challenge the existing mental model of private transportation, kicking off counterfactual thinking that led him to found Turo, the world's first private-car-sharing company.

The idea for 23andMe, a genetic testing company, was also inspired by frustration. The founder, Anne Wojcicki, had

The Parasympathetic Nervous System

In business we often rely on our sympathetic, or fight-or-flight system, that evolved to help us in high-pressure situations, like running from a predator. This system narrows our focus. Less emphasized is the parasympathetic, or rest-and-digest system, which evolved to manage mental and bodily operations when we are relaxed.[a] We can imagine, in hunter-gatherer days, the mental intensity of the hunt followed by time back at home, reflecting on the day's stories, perhaps imagining how to hunt better. We need to create the equivalent rhythm of action and reflection in business to inspire imagination.

I'm not sure that letting him tell stories after every hunt is really working . . .

The sympathetic nervous system is not bad: it helps us block out irrelevant information and makes us anxious to succeed, which is great for well-known or automatic tasks. But as David Rock, director of the NeuroLeadership Institute, observes: "Threat makes you productive . . . if you don't have to think broadly, widely or deeply. A threat response, which we might think of as stress, increases motor function, while it decreases perception, cognition and creativity."[b] Neuroscience is still exploring the ways both nervous systems interact to influence cognition, but one review notes that "the parasympathetic nervous system is critical for higher-order behavior and cognition due to the high-degree of interconnectedness between neural and peripheral structures regulating behavior and physiological state."[c] That is, our brain and body are interconnected; when our body is resting and digesting, it can help our brain with certain higher-order functions. Another study notes that "greater parasympathetic activity is a marker of increased cognitive capacity."[d]

From another perspective, neuroscientist Mary Helen Immordino-Yang has studied the experience of "wakeful rest," or time apart from immediate demands. In a paper called

spent ten years working in health-care investing. At a conference about insurance reimbursement, Wojcicki remembers thinking: "All these people were at this meeting just to figure out how to optimize billing . . . And I just realized, I'm done. It was that moment where I was like: 'The system's never going to change from within.'" This frustration was a

potent emotional mixture, but it took a triggering event for Wojcicki to come up with a better alternative. "There was a very specific event where I was at a dinner with a scientist," she recalled. "We said, theoretically if you have all the world's data and you have all the genetic information, all the phenotypic information, could you solve a lot of questions?

"Rest Is Not Idleness," she argues that this state of mind is essential for "making meaning of new information and for distilling creative, emotionally relevant connections between complex ideas," in particular, "imagining the future."[e] And as psychologist and writer Susan Blackmore commented when we interviewed her: "I'm balking at the idea that we need more stimulation for imagination when I suspect we need less."[f]

To build businesses that support imagination, we should focus on balancing stress and deadline-driven work with supporting our rest-and-digest system. We can use any perks our company might offer: office gardens, wellness rooms, meditation and yoga, lunches, even at-work showers or a simple quiet space. These are often seen as luxuries; instead, we should see them as tools to support inspiration. We should advocate for and utilize such physiology-shaping tools to get ourselves regularly to a state of wakeful rest, free of urgent threats.

I must say, I'm looking forward to switching my rest-and-digest system on tonight . . .

NOTES

a. Ryan J. Guiliano et al., "Parasympathetic and Sympathetic Activity Are Associated with Individual Differences in Neural Indices of Selective Attention in Adults," *Psychophysiology* 55, no. 8 (2018).

b. Judy Martin and Kristi Hedges, "Employee Brain on Stress Can Quash Creativity and Competitive Edge," *Forbes*, September 5, 2012, https://www.forbes.com/sites/work-in-progress/2012/09/05/employee-brain-on-stress-can-quash-creativity-competitive-edge/#399a3893b3e9.

c. Ryan Smith et al., "The Hierarchical Basis of Neurovisceral Integration," *Neuroscience & Biobehavioral Reviews* 75 (2017): 274–296.

d. Giuliano et al. "Parasympathetic and Sympathetic Activity."

e. M. H. Immordino-Yang, J. A. Christodoulou, and V. Singh, "Rest Is Not Idleness: Implications of the Brain's Default Mode for Human Development and Education," *Perspectives on Psychological Science* 7, no. 4 (2012): 352–364.

f. Susan Blackmore, video interview by BCG Henderson Institute, June 24, 2020.

And the conclusion was yes, you would revolutionize health care." This conversation inspired her to begin imagining a new business, a path that eventually led to a genetic testing company with a multibillion-dollar valuation.

Many pieces of information—conversations, observations on a bike—pass us by if we don't care about them. By taking our aggravations seriously, we prepare our minds to be triggered, to imagine our way out of frustrations.

NOTE AND TREASURE ASPIRATIONS

Holding on to aspirations is another way to increase your chance of getting productively surprised. We can see this in

Oh yes, we'll rebuild. Mr. Wolf assures us it was all a misunderstanding.

the case of investor Bill Janeway, special limited partner of Warburg Pincus and economist at Cambridge University. Janeway was one of the leading venture capitalists operating during the rise of mass market computing. In the 1980s, he was driven by the aspiration to upend the then-dominant market for IBM's large, custom-made mainframes. As he told us, "By the late eighties, I was really convinced, distributed computing had the potential for disrupting the main commercial computing markets, which were a decimal order of magnitude larger."[11] This aspiration led Janeway to have conversations with distributed computing start-ups, leading to surprises that further challenged his mental models—starting points for imaginative and successful investments.

An initial aspiration is often unformed: merely the belief in the potential of something or a general desire. But the aspiration helps us notice surprises that prompt us to imagine something more specific—in Janeway's case, ideas for particular investments and new business models he helped to shape.

It can be difficult to take our own aspirations seriously, often because we cannot see anything immediate to do with them. The key, however, is to hold them in mind, to tolerate the uncomfortableness of having a desire without yet having a way to act on it. The aspiration will at some point prompt us to explore new possibilities.

ENGAGE WITH OTHERNESS

To encounter surprise, you not only have to care—you have to be in a position to notice imagination-provoking things. The most basic way to do this is to get out of the (metaphorical) house and seek the unfamiliar. Value contact with otherness.

As a company grows, more mental space becomes taken up with internal requirements: "What happens next in this HR process?" "What should I say to the board?" "How should I write this review?" Like a sphere, the volume of a growing corporation grows faster than the area exposed on the surface. On the inside, familiar processes and scripts come to dominate, shielding us from unexpected and potentially inspiring external interactions.

Sociologist Ronald Burt studied the origins of ideas within companies and found that people who had more exposure to the outside had better ideas. When his study asked inward-facing managers at an electronics company for their ideas, they often produced the "classic lament from bureaucrats—we need people to adhere more consistently to agreed-upon processes." In contrast, what might seem to be the rather routine role of purchasing manager produced imaginative thinking: "Better ideas came from the purchasing managers, whose work brought them into contact with other companies."[12]

To see how easy it is to default to an internal focus, compare two kinds of meetings:

- *A meeting in a large established company.* The team discusses store redesign; the meeting is entirely focused on internal matters: the team's opinions, what a manager wants, troublesome people in another department.

- *A meeting in a vibrant startup.* The team discusses a conference they attended; conversation focuses on external matters: discussions with venture capitalists, opinions they heard from various people about their business. This prompts rethinking of the business: new mental models of how to grow and transform.

Selim of Arabesque describes how he tries to break his team's routines while traveling, to seek encounters that might prompt imagination:

> We all go economy, or take public transport in different countries. Not really for saving money, but to get out there, to have some chance encounters—sitting next to a lady on the train in India who is going to talk to you about her kids, or whatever it may be. When I'm visiting a new city, I have a policy for myself: try to find a meal for under $10. It takes me to some fascinating places, and just gets my mind working—dealing with places, people, or ways of doing things that are not just what I see every day. It often sparks new thoughts.[13]

Another way to encounter surprising otherness is through customer research. Rather than getting analysts to summarize the results, business leaders should observe, or even participate in, the raw discussion with focus groups for the sake of prompting their own imaginations.

Further actions to increase contact with otherness include:

- Have a discussion dinner around an interesting question with external collaborators.

- Attend external events and get others' views on challenges you face.

- Have a meeting focused entirely on things happening outside the company.

- Build relationships with interesting thought leaders to be exposed to new information and mental models.

Daddy thought it would be more imagination-provoking if Mr. Jones from the legal department spoke to us over dinner tonight.

Comprehending

REFLECT ON ACCIDENTS

Another way to find surprises that prompt imagination is to reflect on accidents: the incidental results of our actions or things we bump into while trying to do something else. These are the surprises that come out of left field, unrelated to the mental model we are working with.

Tim O'Reilly, founder of O'Reilly Media and a leading thinker in Silicon Valley, emphasized to us the importance of being open to what might arrive from outside your mental model: "Think of imagination as a process of letting go of what you know, experiencing life fresh. The world is infinite. We experience only part of what is out there. And then, we attach labels to our experience. And people get stuck in the labels. They don't get to their experience without going back and seeing the world [without labels]."[14]

The classic example of this in business is the origin of Viagra. Originally developed as a heart medication by Pfizer, researchers noticed a side effect in a completely different area of the body. This would have been easy to dismiss as a useless side effect; their minds were focused on heart conditions. However, they thought about the accident and connected it with an aspiration from a different medical field: addressing erectile problems. They let themselves be led down this unexpected path, imagining a new therapeutic intervention, and Viagra eventually became one of Pfizer's most successful products.[15]

Another example of productive letting go in business is the origin of the bra. In early 1900s New York, dressmakers Enid Bissett and Ida Rosenthal had an idea for a new kind of dress, one with built-in breast supports. Their aim was to free women from having to wear corsets. Yet when they started selling these dresses, some customers made an unusual request: they asked for *just* the breast supports, without the dress. This feedback would have been easy to dismiss. Bissett and Rosenthal had a new mental model that was getting traction: the all-in-one dress. It sounded as if the customers were just stuck in the old model—wanting something basically like a detachable corset. What made them great business leaders is that they could mentally let go of their commitments, and current labels, and think afresh based on this information from outside their model. They could ask themselves, "What if we did create a detachable brassiere?"

"What if the interesting territory was in fact around the mental model we have been moving away from: recombinable, modular clothing, instead of the all-in-one?"

Entrepreneur magazine writes that Bissett and Rosenthal "didn't set out to become bra manufacturers, and stumbled onto their fortune almost by accident."[16] There was a lot of work to get from their inspirational moment to forming the Maidenform Bra Company and founding today's multibillion-dollar bra industry. But the initial trigger came from thinking about a little piece of information from left field—letting their minds be productively thrown off course by it.

INVESTIGATE ANOMALIES

Another route to surprise is to investigate anomalies. If an accident is something incidental to what you are trying to do, outside the mental model you are working with, an anomaly is a violation of the expectations that a familiar mental model is giving you.

It takes effort to notice this dissonance, to realize that the explanations your mental model suggests are misleading or wrong. As philosopher John Armstrong noted to us: "We're actually quite slow to notice new pieces of information. We have internal resistance, of which we are probably unaware, but which has the effect of blocking things out that might surprise us. It's because our imagined picture is playing a certain emotional role in our lives. We're *invested* in the models we currently have—of a company, of another person, of how things work. And the emotional familiarity is something we can be very reluctant to give up."[17]

One example of successful anomaly investigation comes from a Boston Consulting Group (BCG) project with a US company that makes diagnostic machines for hospitals. The prevailing mental model of this business was to invest in salespeople and save money on technicians. During the project, one executive noticed that the company was selling more machines in Manhattan. This was a crucial moment. It would have been possible to *see* this but resort to the explanation from the prevailing mental model: the sales team there must be better. However, the leaders pushed further to comprehend this thoroughly. In digging deeper, they discovered an additional anomaly: Manhattan was the only region that assigned on-site technicians. The reason for this was that managers didn't want engineers wasting paid hours in New York traffic; it was more efficient to appoint on-site engineers.

The surprise came from connecting the two anomalies. As the team noted, "Constant contact with the technician bred close relationships with the users of the equipment, and the service engineers developed an in-depth understanding of customer needs. Technicians had become the company's most productive salespeople."[18] This surprise kicked off much counterfactual thinking. The leaders imagined a new model for the business. Technicians, who had been marginal to the company's thinking, became central in this model: the business invested in data gathering from technicians and lines of communication between sales and engineering. It assigned on-site engineers elsewhere. Their model was transformed and the result was an additional eight points of market share and a boost to its margins of 25 percent.[19]

"Bubbles," Henri?!
No wine has bubbles.
It is worthless!

We are used to pattern recognition, but the skill of anomaly (or pattern-break) recognition is just as important in business. For pattern recognition, we should think like statisticians. For anomaly recognition, we should think like novelists, who find surprise by looking deeply into the particular. For example, we could regularly pick one unusual sales transaction or customer feedback call and discuss it in depth. Or we could set up a weekly meeting to dig into an anomaly from anywhere in the business, exploring the mechanisms behind it. Such discussions are often fruitful sources of inspiration.

Interpreting

DRAW ANALOGIES

As well as seeing and comprehending, another way to encounter more surprise is by interpreting: exploring the ramifications of a piece of information. You can do this by drawing analogies: taking some element you have comprehended in one area and importing it into another.

Using analogies can be a powerful trigger for imagination in business. The inspiration for car-sharing company Turo came as Shelby Clark—cycling through the snowstorm asking, "Why can't I get in that car?"—drew an analogy:

> I had just come out of a really amazing experience at Kiva.org. It's a peer-to-peer micro-finance lending platform. And I just saw the connection, it made sense: Kiva—a peer-to-peer marketplace—and Zipcar. It just came together right away in my head. The limitation of Zipcar was that there weren't enough cars. Whereas in reality, especially in America, we have a lot of cars. There is no shortage of cars. The problem is that we don't use them well. So a peer-to-peer marketplace would bring people together and solve that problem.[20]

Venture capitalist Bill Janeway also kick-started his imagination with an analogy during the dot-com bubble burst in the early 2000s. As he said, "I wrote my PhD thesis on 1929 to 1931. So in 1999, I had in my mind that stock price chart of RCA between 1926 and '32, and if you put that next to the stock price chart of Veritas between 1996 and '02, they are identical."[21] He told us that seeing this analogy triggered him to adjust his mental model of what could lie ahead and to anticipate the burst of the dot-com bubble.

We don't often search consciously for new analogies, but we could. At the BCG Henderson Institute, we built a library of concepts and mental models drawn from outside business to help with this.[22]

To mine an analogy, use the following process:

1. *Connect.* Identify mental models connected to what you are considering. To draw this connection, describe the features of what you are considering in a more general way. For example, say you are looking for analogies around real estate agents. Real estate agents help people choose houses. This is one instance of the general idea of giving guidance. To find interesting connections, ask: Where else does giving guidance occur? Counseling, advice columns, IKEA furniture manuals, teaching, and so on.

2. *Select.* Choose a concept from a new mental model to import. For example, you might select the concept of *emotional understanding* from counseling (that counselors learn the unique psychology of their clients). Or the concept of *mentoring* from teaching (that teachers relate to their students over time to help them develop).

3. *Inject.* Now explore injecting this foreign concept into the mental model of the original thing. Asking "what if" questions can help prompt your imagination here. What if real estate agents became like counselors in terms of *understanding the emotions* of their clients? What if estate agents became like *mentors*, helping us develop our homes?

Drawing such connections can seem odd, because they are new. But going through this process can offer surprising suggestions that inspire us to start thinking imaginatively, exploring mental models of things that do not yet exist.

LEARN NEW WORLDVIEWS

To increase surprise, you can also learn new worldviews: systems of concepts and mental models that provide different ways of interpreting the world. New worldviews can create surprise when brought up against familiar information. For example, if you hired a manager of a Formula 1 technical crew into the company's logistics team, they might make interesting observations, seeing unexpected ways to rethink or improve the company's logistics, as they notice things through the lens of a worldview developed in high-intensity racing.

Janeway argues for the value of humanities-based worldviews, from philosophy, history, and literature, to enrich the business mind. By living mentally in alternative worlds—scholastic debates in medieval Europe, the life of an aristocrat in nineteenth-century South America, or philosophical thought experiments—Janeway believes we can see with a deeper understanding, allowing us to notice more patterns and anomalies. As he told us:

> We can learn a lot about the emotional elements of financial market behavior from the humanities. A prime example is Anthony Trollope's classic novel, *The Way We Live Now*. It traces an extreme speculative bubble on the London Stock Exchange in the 1870s, promoted by a plausible con man and driven by waves of investors drawn into the fraud until—ultimately and necessarily—the bubble bursts. Our recent history

replicates the phenomenon with extraordinary precision, from Enron through Theranos and on to Wirecard.[23]

Janeway reflected on his humanities education: "I think this background has given me a number of really unfair benefits and advantages as an investor: to be able to have useful, speculative conversations, assess unusual ideas, think about alternative futures."[24]

Visual art also offers us worldviews that help us see surprises. Jane South, chair of the fine arts department at the Pratt Institute in New York, told us:

> In art school we make observational drawings. This is not only to teach people how to draw, but how to look, to *notice*. I say to students: you will never be bored again, if you can learn to extract things from their enmeshed functionality, to see them as *things*, with formal, material, phenomenological properties. Everything that you then encounter, a lamp, a building, a piece of paper will reveal all of its properties. Most importantly you will see *how* you see. You will be able to de-enmesh your own experience and break it down into the multiple strata it actually is.[25]

Such lenses on the world must come on top of core business worldviews, of course. But the worldviews that drive business efficiency can sit alongside the worldviews that help with counterfactual thinking—combined in the mind of a leader who keeps the machine running, while also drawing on deep and broad learning to explore possibilities and new paths to growth.

Pick a few new worldviews to immerse yourself in. They could be from different disciplines, like engineering, logic, theology, or psychology; from writers with distinctive ways of seeing, like science fiction or heroic novels; or from distant places or times that had ways of interpreting that seem strange to us. The point is to enrich your stock of worldviews to draw upon when observing: to expand the range of what you can notice and thus the frequency of imagination-prompting surprises.

What Blocks Inspiration?

As well as actions to take, it is worth examining common blocks to noticing and caring about surprises at the individual level. Many of these are familiar habits that large organizations in particular inculcate in people. We need to be aware of these so we can work to avoid them.

Busy Is the New Stupid

This is the pathology of competing to be busy, which cuts time for reflection and thus the opportunity to encounter surprise. The solution: remember that filling up your calendar, with no room for reflection, is actually an inefficient way to use your brainpower. Your brain can do more valuable things than busywork, even though those valuable things might sometimes appear as merely wandering around or staring out the window. As Bill Gates noted, "It is not a proxy of your seriousness that you filled every minute in your schedule. . . . You control your time, and sitting and thinking may be a much higher priority."[26] It is precisely during the busy times that we should not forget to stare out the window.

Having Only Answers, Not Questions

Pressured perhaps by the social norm in business of appearing prepared and confident, we often want to be the person with the answers—or with questions we only ask because we already know the answers. This means we avoid being surprised. The solution is to sometimes ask questions to which there are no preexisting answers. Good questions take us into unknown or less-known territory, increasing the chance of noticing surprises.

Deprioritizing Curiosity

Curiosity may seem like an indulgence, probably for two reasons: there is usually no immediately valuable outcome, and the eventual outcome cannot be predicted. Yet when we forget curiosity, we reduce our exposure to novelty and our opportunity to notice surprises. The solution: sometimes do things only for curiosity's sake. In

Curiosity? An indulgence??

contrast to a business culture where people only steep themselves in familiar domains of knowledge to support goals set

in advance, you might occasionally be found reading Schiller's *On the Aesthetic Education of Man*, or the *Journal of Geology and Mining Research*.

Overengineering the Environment

This is the mistake of being completely opposed to randomness and chaos. You have your normal routine, normal mode of transport, normal people you interact with, all of which promote efficiency but reduce accidents and anomalies. Too much disorder can undermine a business, which, after all, is an attempt to organize effort in valuable ways. But the solution to overengineering is to balance order with *some* unpredictability in your environment and inputs, for example, varying your routines, spending time with more distant connections in your network, or observing parts of the business

Yes, but Mom, I didn't want to overengineer my environment!

you wouldn't normally see, like a retail outlet or regional office. Remember there is a trade-off between standardization and surprise.

Focusing Only on Averages and Aggregates

We often neglect to examine intriguing individual data points—a unique failed or successful sale, an idiosyncratic sales branch, a single interesting customer—in favor of looking at averages. This blocks exposure to anomalies. Averages are useful in trying to summarize the impact of a complex effort, but we should remember to give anomalous outliers, which may constitute change signals or sources of inspiration, enough attention, too.

Games to Play

Another way to generate triggers for counterfactual thinking is to play some thoughtfully designed games. A game sets an artificial frame, but through it we can discover genuine surprises that spark our imagination.

The "What Do You Think I Think You Are Going to Say?" Game

You can play this game to move yourself off familiar paths of thinking around some topic. The next time you have an important discussion with your team, throw in this question:

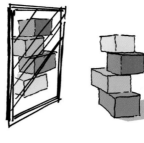

"What do you think I think you are going to say? Now tell me something different." In other words, "Say something that I don't expect that extends the discussion." This question can bump the conversation down new paths, some of which might provoke imagination.

The Bad Customer Game

The ultimate business anomaly and source of frustration is a bad customer. But how often does your business really learn from its bad customers? You can play this game with colleagues to turn a difficult customer into a source of inspiration.

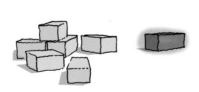

Find some way to meet or hear from the customers who are unsatisfied with your products or services or who have major problems with your business model. You might meet them in person or listen to feedback from customer service calls. Try to understand their needs and motivations. Then articulate the aggravations these people have with your company. Address the question, "What would our business have to look like to be able to satisfy these customers?"

When reconsidering its business strategy, insurance broker and risk manager Willis Towers Watson (WTW) wanted to look at services in the insurance market that could become significant in the future. When it asked its current customers, "Are you happy with what WTW is selling you?," it received mostly positive responses. Then it changed the question to, "What are the frustrations in your economic life and would you go to WTW for help with these?" The answers were less gratifying but more useful. By actively seeking out frustrations, WTW learned about areas of need no one in the market was addressing or ones where the company was not currently offering a solution—a precursor to imagining new products and services.

The Wrong Meeting Game

As a way to nudge yourself and colleagues to encounter new inputs, play a game of going to the "wrong" meetings on a particular project—ones you are not expected to go to, that you are only indirectly connected with. If you are involved in the steering group, skip that meeting for a week and join the technical team's Monday briefing, the marketing group's discussion, or the purchasing managers' check-in. Enjoy turning up in some random places to see if you encounter any different mental models that spark your own rethinking.

Er . . . It's the marketing department. I think they've _all_ come to the wrong meeting . . .

Good Questions to Ask

Questions are often a great starting point for prompting your mind; having a pocket list of questions can help shift your attention in a more fruitful direction. In chapters 3 through 8, we distill the content down to list of guiding questions. These are questions that can cue receptivity to surprise:

- Am I being _too_ efficient and am I reflecting enough?
- What is the biggest aggravation for customers in our business model?
- In a perfect world, what aspirations for the business would I pursue?
- Why did this go right or wrong (useful accidents)?
- What _doesn't_ fit here (anomalies)?
- What is this an example of (analogies)?

Organizational Diagnostic

As a starting point for building a more imaginative company, we should assess our current organization to determine if we as leaders are creating an organizational environment conducive to getting inspired.

There are two utilities to this exercise: knowing where you stand and knowing what to focus on next. To bench-mark your score against other organizations, please visit www .theimaginationmachine.org. To help you identify areas to focus on, each statement in the table below is drawn from an action described in this chapter. If you score poorly on a particular question, you can look to the relevant action as a starting point.

	Related action	Never	Rarely or less than once a year	Sometimes or once a month to once a year	Usually or once a week to once a month	Always or more often than weekly
		(1)	(2)	(3)	(4)	(5)
Employees at our firm regularly make time for quiet reflection.	Make time for reflection					
People in our firm find inventive ways to address problems and frustrations.	Pay attention to frustrations					
The business gives employees regular opportunities to encounter enriching, thought-provoking things outside the firm and its regular clients.	Engage with otherness					
Employees notice, report, and discuss interesting accidental or unexpected outcomes of initiatives or analysis.	Reflect on accidents					
If people in our firm find an unexpected opportunity, they explore how to act on it.	Reflect on accidents					
Our business regularly looks for and analyzes anomalies in granular data.	Investigate anomalies					
People in our firm use surprising analogies and perspectives in presentations.	Draw on analogies					
TOTAL						

After you have added up your total, score your current situation:
31–35, excellent; 21–30, good; 11–20, moderate; 0–10, poor.

Chapter Four

THE IDEA

We might encounter inspiring accidents, anomalies, or analogies, but these won't amount to much if we don't put effort into developing an idea. Consider Charles Merrill, who cofounded Merrill Lynch. After moving on to focus on his role as a director of Safeway—the supermarket chain he helped make successful throughout the Great Depression—Merrill returned as CEO of Merrill Lynch with an imaginative idea for transforming the bank into something like a supermarket. He wanted to reach the middle classes instead of the financial elite, with products and pricing schemes everyone could understand.

Merrill "worked late into the night for a whole month" developing this idea.[1] As his colleague Winthrop Smith recalled: "We went backwards and forwards over the figures and spent hours discussing the possibilities . . ."[2] We spoke to Winthrop Smith Jr., Smith's son and former executive vice president of Merrill Lynch, who explained:

> Merrill talked about putting the customer's interest first. That was how he viewed the chain store grocery business—bringing high-quality goods at a cheaper price to the middle-class person. And he carried that principle into brokerage. They saw that the existing model didn't focus on the client. It was filled with conflicts of interest. And the people weren't very professional; basically they were hired off the street and suddenly they were brokers. They had high fixed costs: beautiful offices and infrastructure that made no sense. He looked at how he ran the chain store at low margins and realized that you could adapt some of that to the brokerage business.[3]

Merrill spent time on counterfactual thinking: imagining what the bank could be. He played with assumptions core to the existing model, asking, "What if brokers were paid on salary rather than commission?" He spelled out the analogy with supermarkets, articulating the Safeway model and the concepts he wanted to import into brokerage services. He considered key constraints, like the lack of trust in banking.

Chapter Overview

Charles Merrill and colleague Winthrop Smith discussing the idea to "bring Wall Street to Main Street." *Source:* Courtesy of Winthrop Smith Jr.

And he connected all the parts into a workable model of a new organization.

What might be a passing thought for most people—that a bank could be more like a supermarket—became a serious model of a possible future, because Merrill developed the idea. Ultimately his reimagined business became the largest securities brokerage in the United States and marked a dividing line between two eras of Wall Street.[4]

• • •

To harness imagination, we need to turn passing thoughts—triggered by surprise—into starting points for rethinking our mental models, in order to develop new, valuable, counterfactual models. This chapter will look at what mental models are, the art of rethinking them, common blocks to doing so, games for practicing the skill of rethinking, questions to ask, and an organizational diagnostic.

What Is a Mental Model?

As described by neuroscientist Karl Friston, "the brain has a model of the world that it tries to optimize using sensory inputs . . . the brain is an inference machine that actively predicts and explains its sensations."[5] In other words, using patterns between neurons, our brain creates miniature, internal systems—mental models—that capture some dynamics of systems in the world. We can have a model of an object, like an office chair, which tells us how the chair works and how it will respond when we interact with it; a model of a person, like a colleague's personality; a model of an organization, such as our business and how it works; as well as models of the entire world or universe and our place in it.

Mental models exist as patterns between neurons, so they wouldn't make much sense to look at directly. But we can make visual representations of them, such as a view of the

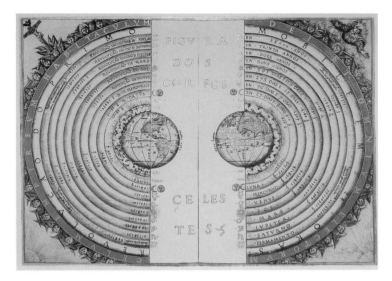

Figure 4-1 Mental model of the world, by Portuguese cosmographer Bartolomeu Velho, 1568

"Figure of the heavenly bodies," an illuminated illustration of the Ptolemaic geocentric conception of the universe. From Bartolomeu Velho's *Cosmographia. Source:* Bibliothèque Nationale de France, Paris. Photo by Alvesgaspar via Creative Commons, 2008.

Earth and surrounding planets—a mental model shared across a whole culture in the 1500s (see figure 4-1).

How do we get the mental models we have? We might imagine that information comes in through our senses and gives us a picture of the world, like light into a camera. In fact, our brains use less sense data than we think. When we walk into a café, we register that it is a café. Then our brain fills in most of what we expect to be there from our idea (model) of what a café is.[6] As cognitive scientist Anil Seth puts it: "We don't just passively perceive the world, we actively generate it. The world we experience comes as much, if not more, from the inside-out as from the outside-in."[7]

Seth describes mental models as controlled hallucinations: "We're all hallucinating all the time, including right now. It's just that when we agree about our hallucinations, we call that reality."[8] The hallucinations are controlled because they are grounded and constrained by sensory impressions as well as other mental models, such as our understanding of the laws of nature. But, especially around more complex models, like a mental model of a business or a country, there is huge scope for rethinking.

One point to note is that in relation to human institutions, the mental model itself becomes part of the dynamics of the system. Unlike the sun, which will keep on being the sun regardless of what we *think* about it, a business is directed and sustained by the mental models of the people who participate in it. When everyone changes their thinking—their mental model of what the business is and should be doing—the business changes. We will explore this later in the book, as we look at the social aspect of imagination: how an imagined mental model creates a new reality by spreading to the minds of others.

Cognitive scientists describe models as made up of beliefs, with probabilities attached. The word "beliefs," however, can be misleading, as we're not always conscious of a mental model's elements or able to articulate them. A mental model is our entire inner representation of something, which includes explicit beliefs, but also images and less articulated emotions and instincts. A professional cyclist has a mental model of the bike and the terrain, which includes beliefs, but

Figure 4-2 Mental model of a home appliances company

also trained instincts (how fast to take corners, what the bike can handle), and mental images (of the landscape and route).

The CEO of a home appliances firm would have a mental model of her company. (See figure 4-2.) This model would include beliefs (about the company's competitive advantage, strategy, or key principles for a lean operation), mental images (of the factories, products, logo, or homes of its customers), and a range of implicit feelings and instincts (about how its customers think and feel, how to be an effective CEO, or the personalities of her top team).

How to Rethink Mental Models

After encountering a surprise—an accident, anomaly, or analogy that challenges our mental models—we might have inspiring but somewhat unformed thoughts, such as:

> What if banks could be more like supermarkets . . .
>
> Could we restructure to give employees more autonomy . . .
>
> I wonder if we could develop a business that brought AI to therapy . . .

How do we go from an open-ended starting point to developing a valuable, counterfactual model? We use our unique human capacities in relation to mental models.

Humans have three unique abilities around mental models. We can reflect on our models as models, treating them as controlled hallucinations and not realities, which opens the possibility for developing counterfactuals. We can be deliberate in our manipulation of mental models, editing, elaborating, and recombining their components to create new models. And we can develop multiple alternative models, allowing us to explore a range of possibilities. We call using these abilities together "the art of rethinking." (See table 4-1.)

Table 4-1 The art of rethinking mental models

See models as models	Manipulate mental models	Develop alternative models
Remember thoughts are not reality	Make mental models explicit	Have a multitrack mind
Remember thinking is free	Play with assumptions	Balance arrogance and humility
Start messy	Mine an analogy	
	Broaden scope and scale	
	Solve for a constraint	
	Connect the parts	

See Models as Models

REMEMBER THOUGHTS ARE NOT REALITY

Because our brains are so good at modeling what's out there—it feels as if our mental model of a table in front of us *is* the table—we often have an unhelpful reverence for our models. Implicitly, we might feel that our idea of a bank is an unchangeable fact, like a piece of the universe that has been there since the beginning. This is how we are taught from an early age, as children's books present us with archetypal images of what exists. (See figure 4-3.)

The feeling that human creations are as permanent as the planets makes it hard to imagine changing them. For instance, we once worked on a consulting project with the CEO of a moderate-size bank, exploring new paths to growth. The discussions focused on extensions of existing operations, for example, selling 7–8 percent more loans in parts of the

giraffe   pluto   bank

Figure 4-3 Mental models can feel like unchangeable parts of reality

agricultural market. It was much harder to discuss counterfactual questions with a broad scope, such as, "What could a bank be?" The assumption was that a bank is a bank—the mental model is fixed—and growth depends on the smart allocation of resources. This approach is workable in the short run, but it misses the opportunity for rethinking what a bank could be. If Charles Merrill had not explored the counterfactual, he would never have discovered an untrodden path to growth and gathered the rewards of rethinking the financial industry.

Every business model was once no more than a mental model. The fact that banks exist now shouldn't make us forget that they are incidental creations, not inevitable. A bank is, at root, an *idea*, an imagined mental model, and it can be reimagined.

A key move, therefore, is to remember that our thoughts do not equal reality. The mental models we live by today are constructed. That means they are full of construction *materials*, to be dismantled, altered, and recombined.

REMEMBER THINKING IS FREE

Another key move to develop an idea is to remember that, other than a little time, playing with mental models costs nothing. Over your career, you've probably had a few fleeting thoughts that would have had huge implications, if pursued. "What if we sold off most of our business?" "What if we moved into a different industry?" "What if we completely rethought the service we provide?" Questions like these are easy to neglect because we fear they suggest complicated, expensive, and perhaps ultimately unwise paths of action.

Don't confuse thinking and rearranging models—a costless exercise—with actually pursuing the changes. Thinking radically is a risk-free activity. We need to give ourselves a chance to construct an exciting alternative reality and discover and articulate its potential benefits before the anticipation of the costs of execution narrows our mind.

Susan Hakkarainen, chairman and CEO of Lutron Electronics, told us how her executive team has a rule to first focus solely on the idea without considering how to implement it:

> A key principle for us is that we don't think about how hard or easy something is, or *how* we're going to end up doing it. We think first about *what* it is. You have to listen to the customer, put yourself in their shoes, listen to what they need, explore the solutions, even if they've never been done before—especially if they've never been done before. The only way to do this is to let yourself rethink, design, build, speculate, tinker, imagine what something could be. Don't *anticipate* what reality is going to throw at you, how difficult it is going to be later. Especially early on in the process, you will probably be wrong anyway. You figure it out later.[9]

START MESSY

Another important move in the art of rethinking is to tolerate the messiness of new mental models, which are often incoherent and unbelievable at first. Good ideas start messy, unclear, unimpressive—even ugly.

Roy Rosin, the chief innovation officer at Penn Medicine, and former head of innovation at the software company Intuit, summarizes this point memorably: "The best ideas are the ones that have had the most chances to evolve."[10]

One example is the origin of the BCG Matrix. The concept is relatively well known as a tool for business portfolio management, but the original sketch is far less easy to understand (see figure 4-4).

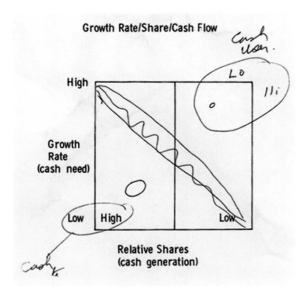

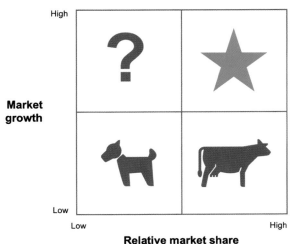

Figure 4-4 The BCG Portfolio Matrix. The starting sketch is always less coherent than the final product

Source: Used by permission of the BCG Henderson Institute, a division of Boston Consulting Group. All rights reserved.

The sketch is a few iterations in, not the first thing he drew, but figure 4-5 shows how the beginning of Twitter looked in founder Jack Dorsey's notepad.

Why do we tend not to be generous with the messiness of early-stage ideas? It is because the origins of great things are often invisible. In the realm of art, this point was articulated in a popular medieval Latin phrase, *ars est celare artem*, "the art is in concealing the art."[11] We encounter a finished poem or painting, and we don't see all the poor drafts and graceless ideas that were discarded to get to that point. Part of the art is making it look effortless. And this holds true in business today. We see the businesses and products that have succeeded; it is not in the interests of their creators to advertise the messiness behind the polished outcome.

To counteract these perceptions, at the BCG Henderson Institute, we have developed a gallery of early-stage mental models to inspire early efforts at rethinking. Because many of these sketches were done on napkins—sitting in a café, at a hotel bar, or over a discussion at lunch—we have called this the "Napkin Gallery." You can access it at www.the imaginationmachine.org/napkingallery.

The key action is to sketch all the pieces that come to mind around your initial inspirational trigger. These starting points might look like fragments on the page, even less coherent than the Twitter drawing: some key words, sketches, a few goals, perhaps back-of-the-envelope calculations. But this is the legitimate and expected beginning of your new mental model—starting messy. We should develop the habit of recording early-stage ideas like this, so they can become explicit, recalled, and evolved over time.

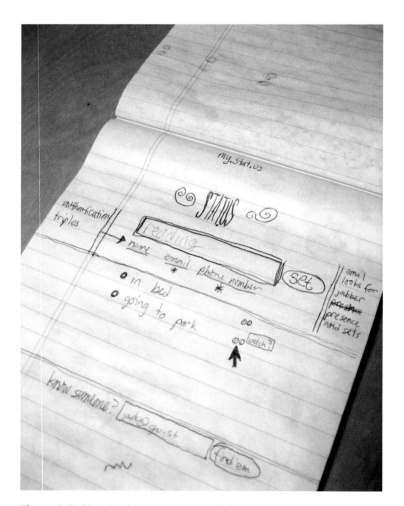

Figure 4-5 Sketch of the elements of Twitter, 2006

Source: "twttr sketch," March 24, 2006, via Creative Commons. Courtesy of Jack Dorsey.

HOSPITAL

GYMS

MEDICATION SCHEDULES

RECOVERY

EMERGENCY CARE

SERIOUS ILLNESS

SELF-IMPROVEMENT

SOCIALIZING

MEMBERSHIP

MEMBERS

SUPPLEMENTS

Figure 4-6 Comparing parts of the mental models of hospitals and gyms

Manipulate Mental Models

MAKE MENTAL MODELS EXPLICIT

Another move in building a new mental model is to identify and articulate all the models connected with your starting thought. Get everything out on the table to see the materials you might want to combine and recombine.

For example, let's say you run a large hospital, and one day at the gym you start imagining a new possibility. Inspired by an analogy—both hospitals and gyms care about health—you start to wonder what it would be like if a hospital became more like a gym.

To take this thought further, you should list and describe the relevant mental models. Articulate the key components of the mental model that currently underpins hospitals or gyms. (See figure 4-6.) You might also write or sketch out other related mental models and their components, such as coaches and nutritionists. (See figure 4-7.)

Figure 4-7 Mental models of coaches and nutritionists

Articulating related mental models gives your imagination, particularly the visual component of it, some pieces to work with, helping you notice new points of analogy and possible recombinations of parts. Pieces of the mental models we live with today are building materials for the models we might live with in future.

PLAY WITH ASSUMPTIONS

Another part of the art of rethinking is playing with assumptions. Assumptions are parts of a mental model that we take for granted—beliefs we feel so certain about that we often forget they are beliefs at all. To develop new models, you can ignore them, tweak them, or reverse them.

For example, Starbucks grew up when the dominant mental model for the coffee business was instant coffee. The assumption was that we had left behind the messiness of ground coffee and noisy espresso machines. And this seemed to be an unstoppable trend. Market leader Nestlé had powerful instant coffee brands and economies of scale.

Starbucks's success was based on reversing these assumptions. Since its founding in 1971, CEO Howard Schultz had focused on the noises, smells, and socializing around espresso machines that he had enjoyed in Italy. He aspired to share this. Starbucks eventually overturned the dominant model of coffee in the industry, but it began with Schultz overturning assumptions in his mind. He played with the assumption that people would always want mess-free, instantly available coffee. Might people enjoy getting ground coffee, if it was still quite convenient, if not instant? Schultz imagined a mental model of a new kind of coffee company (new to the West Coast of the United States), which is still essentially the model of the company today.

Like Schultz, you may find it helpful to return to your aspirations or frustrations, as these can guide you toward which assumptions to rethink. Media entrepreneur John Battelle, cofounder of *Wired* magazine and the Web 2.0 Summit, uses a question to prompt his mind in this direction: "Wouldn't it be cool if . . . ?" Asking the subjunctive question with the word "cool" links the effort to our aspirations: we're not just

I'm rethinking the model of being a giraffe.

playing speculatively with random assumptions; we're asking what pieces of mental models we would find it *exciting* to overturn—connecting the effort with our desires for a less frustrating or better reality. As Battelle notes, "Almost every business I've started starts with, 'Wouldn't it be cool if . . .' and then you let yourself explore something you would like, and imagine in more detail what it could be."[12]

MINE AN ANALOGY

A central move in mastering mental recombination is to get good at mining analogies. As discussed in the previous chapter, analogies can create surprise, triggering imagination. But they can also help us with rethinking and developing mental models.

Imagination and Imagery

When we tend to think about mental models in conceptual terms, labeled with words; we might set out to reimagine the mental model of a bank, which is made up of ideas or concepts of money, debt, accounts, and so on.

Yet one intriguing possibility is that in the early evolution of imagination, the capacity for imagination was based around images, before language evolved.[a] Much of the thinking around this topic is speculative, but there are a few strands of evidence that suggest this.

Our ancestors, at the time of the emergence of genus *Homo* 2.5 million years ago, were visually oriented creatures. Like their primate ancestors, they relied on vision to navigate the world, more than other mammals who relied on smell. For a long time, they developed tools, and perhaps rituals, before the emergence of language. Shells have been found in Trinil, Indonesia, with patterns carved on them from 500,000 years ago, and figurines have been found from 230,000 years ago.[b] Language appears not to have arisen until 100,000 years ago.[c] So there seems to have been a period, lasting hundreds of thousands of years, when our ancestors created—and perhaps communicated with, in some way—visual representations and motifs, before they had the grammar of language.

We can't know whether they developed mental images of nonexistent things before creating them in the world. But it could be that the beginnings of imagination were solely pictorial; that early counterfactual mental models were made of recombined images, rather than concepts labeled with words, as we think of them today. As cognitive science is discovering, higher conceptual cognition is entwined with the visual (as well as emotional and motor) systems.[d] Conceptual thinking partly depends on, and is informed by, mental imagery. This would explain why images are central to imagination. We talk about developing a vision (not a soundscape) of a future company, for example. We say, "Paint me a picture of what you are imagining," meaning, "Give me an image in my head." And the link is there in the word, "image"-ination, and the Latin root *imaginatio*: the act of picturing mentally.

This background can remind us to draw on a visual mode of thinking when we are reimagining mental models. Psychologist and writer Susan Blackmore described to us what goes on in her mind when she is thinking:

I'm constantly speculating on: What are the ultimate constituents of the universe? How on Earth can a brain "give rise to"—I don't even know if that's the right phrase—a thought, let alone the phenomenon we call consciousness. I mull over these things endlessly. I think you would have to say it involves imagination. Some of it is thinking in words about things that I might write, or arguing in my head with somebody else, but the vast majority of my thinking is structural, if you like: I explore patterns and relationships visually, in some kind of imagined space.[e]

Psychologist and engineer J. C. R. Licklider, who worked at the US Defense Advanced Research Projects Agency in the 1960s, was probably the first to imagine a computer desktop, back when computers were clunky calculating machines. It all came from a powerful mental image: "a graphics display that allowed you to see the model's behavior—and then if you could somehow grab the model, move it, change it, and play with it interactively—the experience of working with that model would be very exciting indeed."[f]

Our brains can do cognitive work in images, which can be just as evocative and information dense as statements. We should remember to play with images just as much as words when exploring counterfactuals.

NOTES

a. Stephen T. Asma, *The Evolution of Imagination* (Chicago: University of Chicago Press, 2017).

b. Kate Wong, "World's Oldest Engraving Upends Theory of Homo sapiens Uniqueness," *Scientific American*, December 3, 2014, https://blogs.scientificamerican.com/observations/world-s-oldest-engraving-upends-theory-of-homo-sapiens-uniqueness/; Kate Wong, "The Morning of the Modern Mind," *Scientific American*, June 2005, https://www.scientificamerican.com/article/the-morning-of-the-modern-/.

c. Michael C. Corballis, "Did Language Evolve before Speech?," In R. Larson, V. Déprez, and H. Yamakido (Eds.), *The Evolution of Human Language: Biolinguistic Perspectives* (Approaches to the Evolution of Language) (Cambridge, UK: Cambridge University Press, 2010), 115–123.

d. L. W. Barsalou, "Grounded Cognition: Past, Present, and Future," *Topics in Cognitive Science* 2, no. 4 (2010): 716–724.

e. Susan Blackmore, video interview by BCG Henderson Institute, June 24, 2020.

f. Jessy Lin, "Rethinking Human-AI Interaction" (blog), June 8, 2020, https://jessylin.com/2020/06/08/rethinking-human-ai-interaction/.

Why are analogies useful? Because the world has so many opportunities to import valuable concepts from one area into another. As philosopher Alain de Botton describes it:

It seems as if the universe is inherently structured as a set of motifs that repeat themselves across fields: that the raindrops on a window will imitate the patterns of a dried-out river bed and the fissures on the surface of Mars will follow some of the same logic as the lines on our palm. We are brought up to think in silos. But we should reach around for analogies from apparently alien but secretly sympathetic domains: biology should be invited to illuminate art, art politics, politics relationships, relationships nature, nature our moods, our moods cookery and so on. The benefits of analogy form an argument for keeping our minds well stocked with knowledge from other disciplines, whatever domain we happen to be in.[13]

Charles Merrill reformed banking because he mined an analogy with supermarket chains. As he stated: "We must bring Wall Street to Main Street—and we must use the efficient, mass merchandising methods of the chain store to do it."[14] When Merrill returned to banking after being a director of Safeway, he imagined a new bank by mining his mental model of supermarkets. The concepts he imported became the pillars of his new model: transparent pricing; easily understood products; low-margin, high-volume strategy; customer research; and mass advertising.

As we explored in the previous chapter, to mine an analogy, first identify a mental model that you can see is related in some way to the model you are considering. Second, select a component of the analogous model that you could import into your original model. Finally, step back and consider what this recombination would imply for your original model.

Let's apply this to our imagined example of rethinking hospitals. Having identified related mental models—gyms, nutritionists, and coaches—we might consider importing concepts into hospitals such as membership, daily routines, and training (see figure 4-8).

We can step back to explore what importing these elements might imply for the mental model hospitals. We could ask:

- What if surgery and internal medicine became a side business for hospitals, and the main business became health coaching?

- Could someone actually look forward to going into a hospital, if hospitals focused on self-improvement as well as coping with sickness?

- Could a hospital—via apps, classes, or augmented or virtual reality—become much more involved in guiding our daily routines?

- What would a hospital be like if people were paying members and felt that it was a part of their identity they could be proud of?

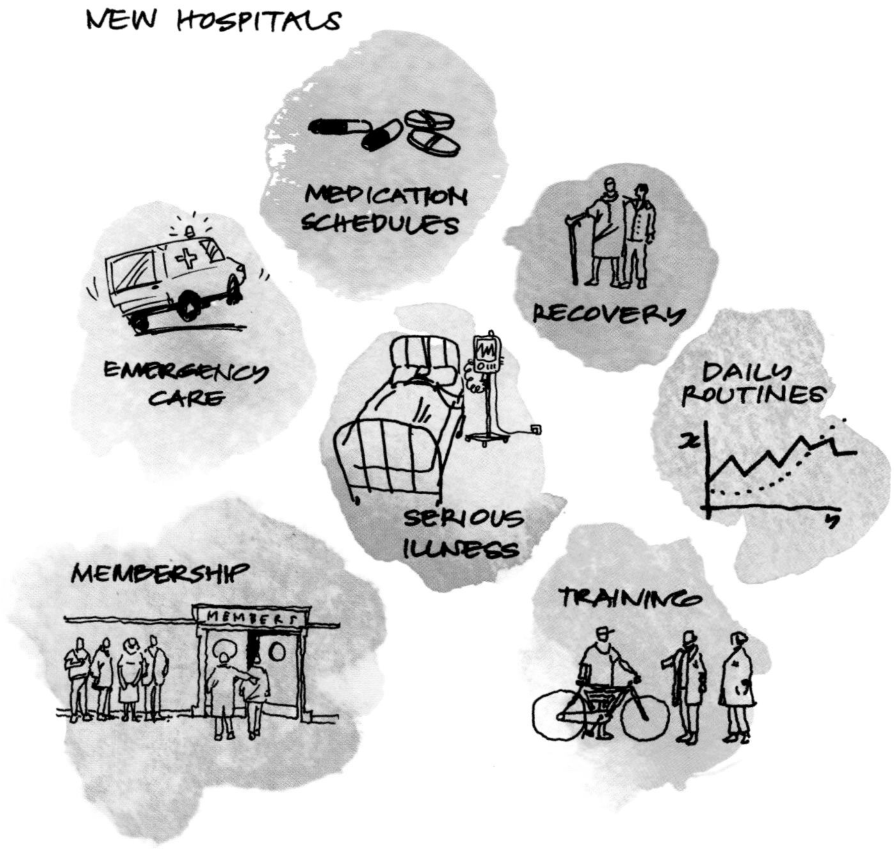

NEW HOSPITALS

MEDICATION SCHEDULES

RECOVERY

EMERGENCY CARE

SERIOUS ILLNESS

DAILY ROUTINES

MEMBERSHIP

MEMBERS

TRAINING

Figure 4-8 Mental model of a new kind of hospital, with elements imported from gyms and coaching

Could a hospital actually be transformed along these lines? We can't know in advance if the particular counterfactuals we explore will lead anywhere, but to be effective at imagining, we have to look past the initial feeling that the things we are combining don't fit together, to enjoy mining analogies and entertaining the possibilities.

BROADEN SCOPE AND SCALE

Another part of the art of rethinking is to expand the scope and scale of the model. This gives us a better chance of capturing the full potential of the possibility we are exploring.

The CEO's last job was in the fishing industry...

the potential new paths to growth we might discover from rethinking. For example:

- *Small version:* Build a film studio that does animated films.

- *Ambitious version:* Build a corporate ecosystem with characters and stories at its heart, with films linked to merchandizing, TV, music, comic strips, theme parks, and a ski resort.

- *Small version:* Introduce customer research and advertising into 1940s banking.

- *Ambitious version:* Reorient banking around mass-mechanizing principles: chains of outlets with low overheads; low prices; and a continuous campaign of educative events, media, and advertising to change the mindsets of millions of people who have never bought securities.

How can we push ourselves to expand the scope and scale of our thinking? One technique is to think back to shifts in history, to recreate in our minds the novelty of ideas that we now take for granted, and to ask ourselves what the successor idea will be.

Take the now very familiar concept of a vacation. This concept seems entirely normal to us, but to anyone before 1700, the mental model would have been outlandish: the idea of traveling halfway around the world to see an old building or lie on a beach. It would have taken a courageous, imaginative person to propose this as an appealing thing to do, let

For example, Walt Disney imagined diversifying his company in the 1950s. Figure 4-9 captures the extent and scope of his thinking.

Ten years later, in 1967, the scope and scale had become even more ambitious, including the idea of a ski resort in Mineral King Valley in California (which was never completed) and a range of other components of a business empire (see figure 4-10).

The smaller version of an idea is often difficult enough to pursue. But expanding the scope of our imagination expands

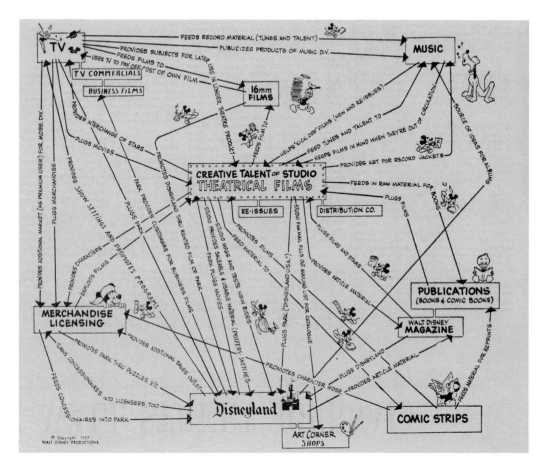

**Figure 4-9 A chart of Walt Disney
Production's synergistic approach, 1958**

This was created by a Disney Studio artist.
This chart first appeared in a 1958 *Wall Street
Journal* article, "Disney's Land; Walt's Profit
Formula: Dream, Diversify—and Never Miss an
Angle: Here's How His Divisions Complement
Each Other," by Mitchell Gordon. *Source:* The
Walt Disney Company. © 1957 Disney.

alone to suggest that millions of people in the future would pay to do this annually. Yet we know that this apparently off-the-wall thinker would in fact have been talking realistically.

The lesson from this, as philosopher John Armstrong said to us, is that "when we look at the past, we can see many, many world-changing things were possible at the time, which people did not realize. We know this. What we forget to tell ourselves is that *this must be true for us in the present as well*. There are many big changes we could introduce to the world—not the trends that everyone talks about, but things

Figure 4-10 An updated Walt Disney Studios chart, 1967

This revised chart appeared in *The Disney World* magazine, July 1967. Included in the description of the chart was the following sentence, "The headline introduced an article describing, in admiring detail, how the various divisions of Walt Disney Productions work in concert, complementing one another both creatively and in the marketing areas. A Disney chart, similar to the one below, helped tell the story graphically." *Source:* The Walt Disney Company. © 1967 Disney.

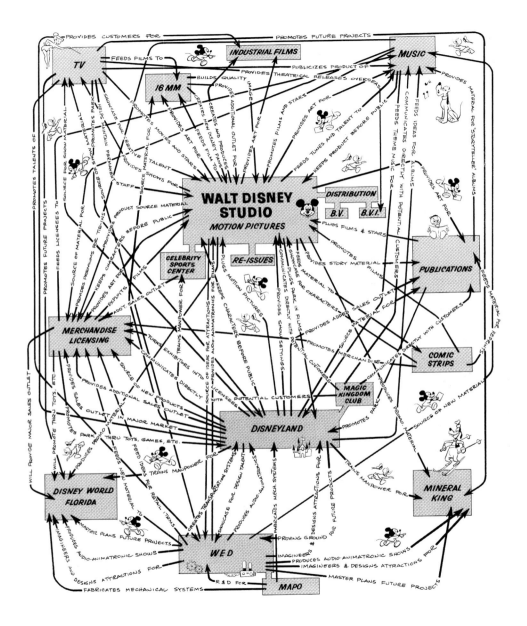

It would have been realistic to tell them that one day, millions of people would pay to leave the country to lie on a beach—but they would have laughed. *Source: David Teniers the Younger (1610–1690), Tavern Scene, 1658. Courtesy National Gallery of Art, Washington.*

must evolve your counterfactual thinking: to adjust a model so that it expands into new areas or to adjust a model so it might work despite an obstacle.

Charles Merrill's aspiration of bringing brokerage services to the middle class faced a big constraint: his new target audience was generally wary of the world of finance. Merrill articulated this constraint in vivid detail—how typical middle American customers might respond to a Merrill Lynch broker or "customer's man": "When we give that man a report on a certain company, he may not tell us, but in the back of his head is a lot of curiosity and a lot of suspicion. He is just wondering all the time, with one-half of his brain, 'How much of this can I rely on? What is behind it? Why should this customer's man show me these facts and figures regarding a company that I never heard of before? What is his motive?'"[16]

Addressing the constraint of lack of trust was an impetus to refine his model, to ground it more in reality. Merrill envisioned reforms focused around securing customer trust: paying brokers a wage rather than a commission; sharing all information with the customer; and voluntarily publishing the bank's corporate finances annually (which no bank did at the time).

As you develop your mental model, you can use constraints to generate questions you challenge yourself to address. For example:

that are not obvious at all—big proposals that sound completely left-field and way too ambitious that are in fact entirely possible."[15]

The history that people will tell in fifty or a hundred years' time is not predictable. We have the ability to shape it, and we should be audacious in our thinking. Dramatic ideas we muse about now might turn out to be the new obvious, normal things for people of the future.

SOLVE FOR A CONSTRAINT

In the art of rethinking, addressing constraints can be as valuable as expanding scope and scale. In both cases, you

- "I want to make it normal to get espresso-based coffee. What would it take to solve for the fact that people are used to getting their coffee instantly?"

It's a new service for our customers.

- "I want to make a hospital that people attend aspirationally, like a gym. What would it take to overcome people's aversion to going to hospitals, especially when they are not sick?"

- "We want to build a theme park. How can we solve the problem that most of our customers cannot afford to travel across the country to visit?"

CONNECT THE PARTS

A final move in manipulating mental models is to step back and connect all the elements. Doing so helps us see the crucial elements that many pieces depend on and identify gaps in our thinking.

Using templates such as the Business Model Canvas developed by Alex Osterwalder can be helpful (see figure 4-11).[17] Although you may not yet have all the answers about the company you want to reimagine, the new product and service you want to develop, or the business you want to build, such templates can prompt you to think about different aspects of your developing model and look at them as an integrated whole.

In the reimagining of Merrill Lynch, Merrill regularly connected the pieces in his speeches to the company, creating a coherent vision (see figure 4-12).

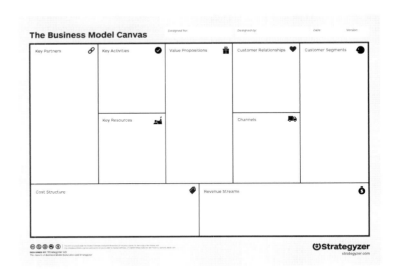

Figure 4-11 The Business Model Canvas, template for a mental model

Source: Courtesy of Strategyzer AG, 2020.

Figure 4-12 Charles Merrill's interconnected mental model of a future bank

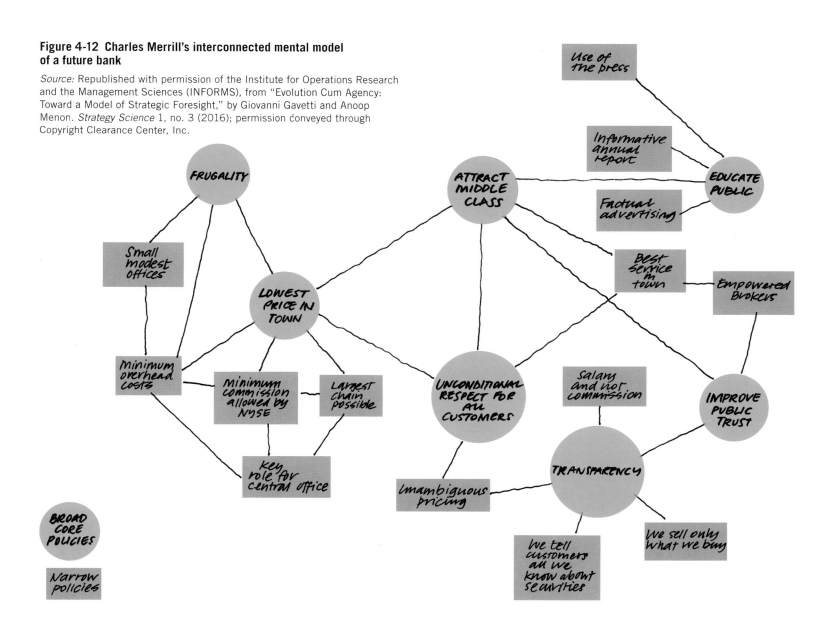

Develop Alternative Models

HAVE A MULTITRACK MIND

Another aspect of the art of rethinking is to allow yourself to develop multiple, alternative new models of your idea in parallel. It doesn't matter if the models contradict each other.

As F. Scott Fitzgerald said, "The test of a first-rate intelligence is the ability to hold two opposed ideas in mind at the same time and still retain the ability to function."[18] We call a mind with the ability to do this a "multitrack" mind.

During the Middle Ages in Europe, when the university system was born, this kind of mind was celebrated. At that time, the primary means of education was not the one-way lecture but the *quaestio disputata*, debate around a disputed question. A key purpose of the debates was for participants to practice being as charitable as possible to the mental models of the other side. The most admired scholars could hold the opposing perspectives in mind and even articulate them better than their proponents. For example, the most well-known scholar of this time, Thomas Aquinas, articulated a position *against* the existence of a divine being: "If one of two contraries were infinite, the other would be destroyed. But God is called the infinite good. Therefore, if God exists, there would be no evil."[19] He put this so pithily, it was cited by atheists making their case during the Enlightenment.

When we lack a multitrack mind like this, we miss the full potential of mental models counter to our favorite one. In business, for example, one reason the now-defunct Polaroid Corporation couldn't take advantage of digital cameras was that the company was dominated by chemists.[20] Their worldview was based around film: a chemically reactive material that responds to light. To them, exposing and developing film was the *definition* of photography. Telling them that photography could be done via computers would be like telling a chef that meals could be pills. It is an entirely different mental model to get one's head around. At Polaroid Corporation, the old mental model was also the basis of the commercial model: cameras were less-profitable, one-off sales; the company made its money from selling film. So, the leaders of the company were reluctant to explore mental models that would challenge this strategy.[21]

The business could have gone down a new path of growth if the executives had had multitrack minds: if they could have held a range of hypothetical models in mind at one time, alongside the chemistry-driven, film-oriented one.

The value of multiple mental models is partly in hedging the risk of betting on one vision of the future, partly in exploring a wider search space, and partly in expanding the capability to do both of these things.

BALANCE ARROGANCE AND HUMILITY

The art of rethinking requires overturning established aspects of the current world (in your mind) and believing that your mental model could shape reality. But it also requires recognizing that models are just models, imperfect, often messy, and perhaps not even possible, which is why we need to develop many of them. It requires us to balance egotism and humility.

The biologist Simon Levin, one of the leading minds who shaped mathematical biology, shared with us some reflections on the appropriate role of ego in imagination: "Most people assume that they're not going to be able to come up with new ideas and just look to others for what they should do. We all do that to some extent, but you have to have enough ego that you're willing to put forth ideas, have confidence in them, and the resilience to push them through to reach a certain level of development."

The danger lies in doing this without countervailing humility, becoming like "those individuals who due to insecurity, are afraid to listen to competing ideas—people that, if they *don't* push their ideas through, feel they've been somehow diminished personally."[22] Levin recalled:

> One of the most important influences on me was the late, great economist Kenneth Arrow, who when you came to him with a problem was known to say, "Well, I don't know anything about that, so therefore I'm really interested in it." He had remarkable expertise, but he had humility. You need people who, despite their achievements, have respect for the other people in the conversation. I can think of good examples of people who don't. Largely because of their insecurity, they insist on imposing their view. These people lack imagination in my view because they're not willing to think about systems in new ways.[23]

Balancing ego and humility involves holding both principles in mind, letting one temper the other so that neither becomes extreme, and letting yourself be led by one and then the other: at one moment, having the ego to push forward a thought; at another, the humility to listen generously to a critic.

What Blocks Rethinking?

There are several common blocks in business that can undermine the potential for initial surprises to lead to powerful new counterfactual mental models.

Impatience with Ideas

A common block is the lack of tolerance for the implausibility of early-stage ideas before they might be worked into something more plausible. It is a lack of patience to persist through the uncertainty of early-stage discussions and the skepticism that new ideas invite. The solution: suspend judgment during the early stages of ideas, when they inevitably seem more confusing and less valuable than they might become with development.

The Desire to Belong

Although our desire to belong is important in building a cohesive company, it can become a detrimental factor when it suppresses entrepreneurialism. When we want to fit in above all else, we become unduly influenced by the collective view of how things work and lose our distinctive perspectives. The solution is to value, or at least tolerate, ideas that depart from the norm, even if the particular case is not valuable; this sends a message to people that part of belonging is to do some things that don't belong.

Defense of the Status Quo

Another block is the tendency to defend the familiar against emerging new ideas, often with  only a veneer of rationality. Behind defensiveness are common fears:

- Fear that rethinking will be too difficult and a waste of time

- Fear of looking stupid when trying to reimagine what is well established

- Fear that the consequences of reimagining things will diminish one's status

This block is difficult to address, as anxieties underpinning the defense of the status quo are often deeply rooted. One solution is to communicate with gripping stories, which we explore in chapter 6. Another solution is to celebrate imaginative proposals, both to reduce the fear of consequences and to demonstrate the legitimacy of rethinking.

Focus on the Concrete

Another block to rethinking mental models is when the dominant habit becomes focusing on the concrete—that is, focusing on what is readily actionable, where there is an apparently safe path forward. From this perspective, people dismiss rethinking as too risky. Such people have an advantage: the metaphor of concrete is appealing; it implies a place to put our feet that we can trust, as opposed to heading into the unknown. Who would dare propose leaving a concrete path? The problem is that what we think of as concrete and safe is not always so. Doing the familiar thing once again might turn out, this year, to be disastrous. Covid-19 might arrive, and because you have never left the known path, you are not prepared to cope. Or, more commonly, doing the safe, readily actionable thing year after year leads to slow decline. This is the fallacy of a false baseline—continuity feels like a much safer course than it might objectively be.

The solution is to see that in the long run, the safest path to success inevitably involves reimagining the business. Everyone wants their next step to be on concrete, but in a changing environment, it's hard to find any permanently stable ground, hence, the necessity of rethinking mental models.

Games to Play

Playing some well-constructed games with colleagues can help free our minds from the models we habitually use to view the world. We have used these games with clients and have found that discussions when we have opened with a game are often more fruitful and insightful than they otherwise might be.

The Invert Your Business Game

Think through your current business model, articulating key underlying assumptions. For example, a car manufacturer's business model is based on the assumptions (1) people want to buy cars, (2) cars will be manufactured in factories, (3) the main offering of the company is cars, and so on. Then change these assumptions, either by reversing them or radically altering them. Make the best case for doing business based on these inverted assumptions.

For example, altered assumptions could include that people only rent cars (that the offering is a service, not a product), or that cars or parts are made by 3D printing and assembled in a decentralized fashion.

The point is to stretch thinking to generate ideas that may be worthy of further consideration. And even if you find no useful ideas immediately, unfreezing the current mental model of the business facilitates subsequent exploration of possibilities. An apparently ridiculous idea might indeed turn out to be unviable—or it may be

merely unfamiliar and uncomfortable from the perspective of your current mental model of the business. You can't discover valuable but uncomfortable ideas without first thinking counterfactually.

There are two intended outcomes of this game. First, to make explicit the assumptions on which your business model is based. Second, to generate ideas from the inverted company perspective that suggest new paths to growth.

The Solving Bigger Problems Game

First, identify the area of your customer's life that your company addresses. For example, Amazon aims to "solve shopping." It has identified an entire area of the customer's life and seeks to help with all the problems in it. For your company, if you were consumer-facing, you might answer "transport," "accommodation," "being organized," "emotional growth," or "relaxing and having fun." As an enterprise-facing firm, you might answer "managing external relationships," "maintaining physical assets," or "keeping employees happy."

Second, forget about what you *currently* do and offer, and think about this entire area of your customer's life. List all the frictions, annoyances, struggles, hopes, desires, and risks that exist in this area of life. For instance, if you were running a bank, you could think of every money-related problem and need that people have, such as feeling disorganized around money; dealing with money-related anxiety; needing to teach children about money; being driven by money but regretting this later; wondering what to save for.

Third, imagine solutions to these problems—whether or not your business or any business has addressed these problems before. For instance, as a real estate company, you could say you are "solving accommodation." This implies more than just helping people buy and sell houses; it could include services that we currently classify under interior design, construction, financing, hospitality, or travel. You might imagine new services to help customers decide when they should move house or figure out what they are really looking for in a home as a function of their life stage and outlook. Use each frustration or aspiration of the customer as a starting point to imagine transforming your company and its offering.

The intended outcome of this game is the evolution of the mental model of your company as a whole—clarifying what area of life you are addressing—and a list of promising ideas for new products and services.

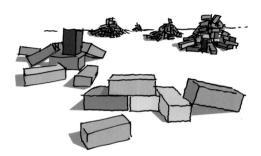

They did say this hotel was known for researching their customers' needs.

- What are the key constraints that stop the current model from being more valuable and what happens if we relax or solve for them?

- What is our business like (what parallels can we draw with anything else in the world or through history)? If we mine the analogy, what new possibilities does it suggest?

- What are the mental models of our most innovative competitors and what can we learn from them?

- What if we doubled our confidence or our humility in rethinking our business?

Good Questions to Ask

The following questions are useful prompts to develop new mental models that might reshape your business:

- What is our current mental model of the business?

- What are the unspoken assumptions of this model?

Organizational Diagnostic

As in the previous chapter, we can assess our organization to see whether as leaders we are creating an environment that is conducive to rethinking. This exercise can help you determine where you stand and which of the actions in this chapter you should focus on next.

	Related action	Never (1)	Rarely or less than once a year (2)	Sometimes or once a month to once a year (3)	Usually or once a week to once a month (4)	Always or more often than weekly (5)
When people at our company discuss their beliefs and perspectives (mental models), they discuss them as though they are hypotheses, open to change and revision.	Remember thoughts are not reality					
In general, employees respond to new ideas by trying to improve them rather than shooting them down.	Remember thinking is free					
People in our firm are patient with unformed, early-stage ideas.	Start messy					
Employees regularly ask "what if" questions.	Play with assumptions					
People in our firm talk speculatively and playfully about potential large changes (in the world or in the company's process, products, or strategy).	Broaden scope and scale					
People in our firm explore topics, analyses, or decisions from multiple, contradictory perspectives.	Have a multitrack mind					
TOTAL						

After you have added up your total, score your current situation: 31–35, excellent; 21–30, good; 11–20, moderate; 0–10, poor. To benchmark your score against other organizations, please visit www.theimaginationmachine.org.

Chapter Five

THE COLLISION

In the early days of the LEGO Group in the 1940s, founder Ole Kirk Kristiansen and his son Godtfred were presented with some plastic bricks invented by a British toy maker, Hilary Fisher Page. (See figure 5-1.)

Kristiansen decided to make a similar brick, initially with a few modifications to the Kiddicraft brick, straightening rounded corners and adjusting the size.[1] (See figure 5-2.)

As the company's history site records: "In the late 1950s, the LEGO Group contacts Kiddicraft to ask whether they object to the LEGO brick. They do not. On the contrary, they wish the company good luck with the bricks, as they have not enjoyed much success with their product."[2] From this point on, the two trajectories were remarkably different. The executive chairman of LEGO Brand Group told us the story:

> It was 1958, and the new managing director, Godt-fred Kirk Christiansen, was sitting in his office with

Figure 5-1 Kiddicraft plastic bricks

Source: © 2020 The LEGO Group.

Chapter Overview

Why do we act?

How can action accelerate imagination?

REFOCUS
- Be monomaniacal
- Create a learning journey

MOVE
- Visit a relevant environment

PROBE
- Probe early
- Probe selectively
- Probe playfully
- Probe iteratively

What blocks action?

IGNORING SURPRISE

NOT ITERATING

RELIANCE ON PERMISSION

OVEREMPHASIS ON ANALYSIS AND DEDUCTION

NOT LETTING GO

Games to play

THE NEWS HEADLINES GAME

THE $100 GAME

Good questions to ask

Organizational diagnostic

Figure 5-2 The Automatic Binding Brick

Source: © 2020 The LEGO Group.

the director of the German sales subsidiary, LEGO GmbH, who mentioned he was getting complaints from customers that the bricks fall apart too easily. This news started a long discussion and brainstorm. At some point, Godtfred found a piece of paper—with circles on it showing a LEGO brick viewed from above, used by the designers for product drawings—and he sketched an idea for a brick with inner clutch tubes.

That same day, he gave the sketch to the head of the molding shop, who made a sample. On his way home, he was still thinking about it, and decided that three inner tubes might be better than two. The next morning he got the molding shop to create another sample by cutting up and gluing together existing pieces. Then he sent the design via express post to the patent

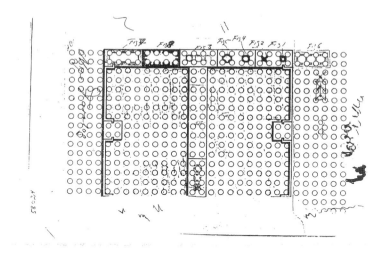

Figure 5-3 Initial sketch for the LEGO® brick stud-and-tube principle
Source: © 2020 The LEGO Group.

office. Within five days they had gone from a conversation to a patent application for the stud-and-tube brick, the toy that came to define the company.[3] (See figure 5-3.)

The Kiddicraft and LEGO businesses were guided by two different philosophies of action. Kiddicraft sought to validate its idea in the marketplace. Being an inventive company with a wide range of toys, it decided that the brick was not particularly successful and so focused elsewhere. LEGO, on the other hand, sought to use the *surprises* that came back to it, in this case, the comment that the bricks fall apart too easily. LEGO persisted, iterated, and was continually open to surprise and how surprise might prompt rethinking. Its

product became more grounded: more usable within the constraints of the world (in this case, gravity). Integrating thought and action, it set up a reimagination loop around its product which Kiddicraft lacked, driving its growth into a billion-dollar company.

• • •

A new mental model remains just an individual indulgence unless we act—to collide the idea with reality, spur our imagination again, and drive the evolution of the idea. Next, then, we will look at taking an idea from the mind to the world and back again, setting up a feedback loop between the world and the imagining brain.

This chapter will examine why we act, how action can accelerate imagination, blocks to action, games to play to enhance the capability to act, questions to ask, and an organizational diagnostic to assess your business along this dimension.

Why Do We Act?

It might seem odd to ask why we act, as business is focused on action. But there are different ways we can think about acting, or colliding ideas, with the world. As we saw with the LEGO Group, the right mentality can make the difference between an idea that never realizes its potential and an imaginative journey along a unique path to growth.

There are two different mindsets we can bring to action. The first is to seek validation of an idea by making it real or testing it out in some way. We usually do this as part of a portfolio of ideas, like Kiddicraft's range of self-locking bricks, plastic eggs, mosaics, threading beads, and miniature groceries. This approach to action is like that of a tree that disperses many seeds to the wind. The hope is that some of the seeds find the right ground in which to germinate. We are looking for a basic response from the world: Did the idea work—did the seed grow—or not?

The other mindset is to look for surprise. This mindset utilizes our imaginative capacity not just in the conception of a product, but iteratively. We look for feedback from the world to spur our imagination again to rethink and evolve the idea. Christiansen got the feedback that the bricks didn't stick together well and sat down to sketch out possibilities, trying them out that day. In this mindset, instead of looking for a binary response from the world—did the idea work or not?—we are looking for the world to disrupt the way we think. This mindset is valuable because of the complexity

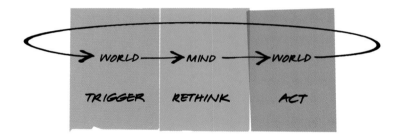

Figure 5-4 Reimagination loop: acting on a mental model creates triggers for further rethinking

of the world; we often forget how little we know and how much the world has to teach us (see the sidebar "Philosophy of Action").

The two mindsets are not mutually exclusive. We should look to validate and evolve at the same time. The danger comes when we forget to be open to surprise as we act in the world and fall into the habit of only seeking validation. When we are open to surprise, we set up a reimagination loop, where action triggers surprise, rethinking, and further action: a continuous interplay between mind and world, which accelerates imagination. (See figure 5-4.)

How Can Action Accelerate Imagination?

If you have a developing mental model in mind, what kinds of action can you take to collide it with the world, to generate further surprise, and further stimulate your imagination? In

Figure 5-5 What to do with an early stage idea: ways of taking our idea to the world

chapter 2 we explored rethinking after encountering a surprise. The other actions involve engaging with the world: refocusing (adjusting your attention), moving to a new environment (adjusting your position), or probing the environment (adjusting the world). (See figure 5-5.) The other action—communicating—takes imagination to a social level, which we will explore in the next chapter and beyond.

Refocus

One subtle but powerful way of bringing your developing mental model into contact with the world is to shift your attention—to deliberately change the focus of your perception and your mental filters.

BE MONOMANIACAL

One key technique for refocusing is to use your mental model as a lens through which to view everything you encounter. We can call this "monomania": a usefully obsessive focus on seeing the world through your new mental model. As mentioned in chapter 3, the inspiration for car-sharing company Turo came about because the founder Shelby Clark drew an analogy with peer-to-peer lending service Kiva.org. This happened because Clark was obsessed with the peer-to-peer model: "Kiva was one of the first places where I got to see the move [in online services] into the offline world.

Philosophy of Action

As neuroscientist Walter Freeman described, our theories of how the brain relates to the world have largely derived from one of two models, both of which began in ancient Greece.[a] On the one hand, there is the tradition of Plato. Here there is no great role for action; Plato focused on using reason to find unchangeable truths about the world. At the beginning of each of Plato's books, the protagonist Socrates is usually just walking around finding a nice place to sit and think. This is the most action that occurs. When Plato thought about the mind perceiving the sensory world, it was in passive terms. Forms from the world (information) enter our senses and are compared by the mind with ideal forms (pattern recognition). This model broadly informed most of cognitive science up until the last couple of decades.[b]

On the other hand, there is a tradition derived from Plato's student Aristotle, which sees action as central to perception and how we relate to the world. As Freeman described, in the Aristotelian view, understanding "requires movement into the world by probing, cutting, and burning in order to learn by manipulation the forms, textures, weights, and appearances of objects."[c] This followed from Aristotle's personal style of engaging with the world. To write his book *The History of Animals*, Aristotle

I'd like to borrow a bee.

cut open many animals, like chameleons and bees, to see what was going on. By fiddling around with the world, he was able to encounter surprises—things that, perhaps, no one had ever noticed before: "If a hair is cut, it does not grow at the point of section, but gets longer by growing upwards from below."[d]

Aristotle emphasizes that action is intertwined with everything the mind does: the intention of every effort is fundamental because it shapes all that follows.[e] This model informs more recent cognitive science, particularly "embodied cognition," which looks at how thinking and perceiving are shaped by how we act in our environment. We know now that when our brain conceives an action, it sends out copies of anticipated motor commands to the *sensory* cortices—meaning that how we intend to act primes the way we see the world.[f]

Neither of these two perspectives, however, provide much of a role for imagination. A third view, developed by Thomas Aquinas based on Aristotle's philosophy, shows the interplay between imagination and action. In Aquinas's view, we interact with the world, generating sense impressions that he calls "phantasms." Unlike Plato's view, and much of cognitive science, Aquinas doesn't see the senses as simply carrying the forms of things into our mind. Rather, he emphasizes the uniqueness and fleetingness of sense impressions, like light sparkling on water. Each phantasm or moment of experience *selects* certain models above others that our brain, our *imaginatio*, generates. As we act in the world, our imagination generates and regenerates the models we use, until they become subtler and richer, closer to the infinite richness and depth of

OK, Jerry, let's get the manual—
I think we've done enough fiddling . . .

reality, Aquinas argued.[g] This view is supported by research that shows our brain creates clouds of neuronal activity, or "wave packets," which are *selected by* sense data, rather than being *built out of* sense data.[h] We might even translate wave packet as an imaginative mental model, being collided with reality, the incoming sense data.

The philosophy of Aquinas can teach us a key lesson. Because the world is complex beyond what any brain can encompass, we create the inner world that works for us, and this inner world develops, and becomes useful, because we act.

This point is captured in the medieval Latin word *intendere*, the root of "intention," which means both "to push the self into the world," and "to grow in understanding." Whether we are making a model more grounded, to navigate how things are, or more ideal, to capture greater possibilities, it is through action—pushing ourselves into the world, stirring up surprises from its many layers—that our models become more subtle, powerful, and useful.

NOTES

a. Walter Freeman, "Nonlinear Brain Dynamics and Intention According to Aquinas," *Mind and Matter* 6 (2008): 207–234.

b. Walter J. Freeman, "Neurodynamic Models of Brain in Psychiatry," *Neuropsychopharmacology* 28 (2003): S54–S63.

c. Ibid.

d. Aristotle, "The History of Animals," Classics Archive, http://classics.mit.edu/Aristotle/history_anim.mb.txt.

e. Roger Crisp, *Aristotle: Nicomachean Ethics* (New York: Cambridge University Press, 2000).

f. Freeman, "Neurodynamic Models of Brain in Psychiatry."

g. Freeman, "Nonlinear Brain Dynamics and Intention According to Aquinas."

h. Freeman, "Neurodynamic Models of Brain in Psychiatry."

It was the concept of connecting people online and offline that was really powerful to me. So, I was actively considering, 'In what other ways can this interesting behavior be applied?' Like housing. That was one area I was thinking a lot about."[4]

Clark was monomaniacal about this: "I was thinking peer-to-peer everything." Refocusing his attention in this way eventually led him to a surprise that prompted a new counterfactual mental model: a peer-to-peer business for sharing private cars.

Let's say you were rethinking what a hospital could be. To practice some useful monomania, you might read a news story about an airline attempting to build trust with customers. This could prompt you to think about building trust with customers around a new kind of gym-hospital business. Or, you might chat with a colleague about going on vacation. This could prompt you to think how your new kind of health company could work with people on vacations. Or, you might be reading a book about the Byzantine Empire. This could prompt you to think about what goes wrong in hospital bureaucracies, and so on. Using your new model as a lens for everything will generate new surprises that will further drive the model's evolution in your imagination.

CREATE A LEARNING JOURNEY

Another way to collide an emerging idea with the world is to engineer the supply of information that comes into focus. We tend to do this naturally. If we are excited by an idea, we might order a few books or discuss it with colleagues. But you can do this more systematically, creating a "learning journey" for yourself, based on your developing mental model.

Build a curriculum for yourself to learn more deeply about the core areas of your mental model and to encounter more imagination-prompting surprises. First, identify a few core themes of your developing mental model. Then think about the key areas of knowledge that touch on these themes.

For example, imagine you were the leader of the LEGO Group in the days after the invention of the stud-and-tube brick. You might have the following themes in your emerging

Figure 5-6 Emerging mental model of the future LEGO®

mental model of the future company: play, plastic, recombination, and continuity (all LEGO products compatible across time). (See figure 5-6.) Based on this, you might pick a few areas of knowledge to dive into, for example, the psychology of play, plastic chemistry, or companies that have built long-lasting, intercompatible systems of products.

You also might push yourself to think more broadly. You could identify a historical precedent that connects in some way with your idea, for example, "toys in ancient China." You could find a few imaginative creations (art, movies, poems, novels) that touch on your developing idea, for example, children's stories or a novel about an inventor. You could look to areas of knowledge even further out from your model, where you might find fruitful analogies: bridge engineering, the science of color, or recombination in evolution.

As you refocus on such areas, the goal is not to find immediately applicable knowledge. It is to set up streams of information to collide with your model, in order to spark new rounds of surprise and rethinking.

Move

In addition to shifting attention, another way of colliding our idea with the world is to move to a different part of it, immersing ourselves in a different geographical or social (customer) environment.

VISIT A RELEVANT ENVIRONMENT

Often, the people doing the imagining and strategic thinking in a project will not be the ones immersed in the environments where the ideas will play out. Yet it is important to ensure that the people who are doing the imagining do participate directly, rather than having the raw experience filtered through someone else. Such filtering, or summarizing, by other people reduces the possibility of surprise.

In 1963, when BCG was a staff of two inside an office twelve feet by twelve feet, the founder, Bruce Henderson, learned this lesson. One of BCG's first projects was on "the buying influences and the pattern of use for paper in the office" of a client (as Henderson put it, "we were really hungry"). They conducted some research interviews as part of this, which they delegated. "We subcontracted some of the interviews to freelance professionals. To validate the information we received, we reinterviewed a sample. The requested data had been faithfully provided, but the important insights had been omitted. The client had not asked us for the really important things we learned."[5] They had taken the client's brief and shared that with freelancers, who conducted interviews. The freelancers gave them back information relevant to the brief. But what Henderson's team missed were moments in interviews that would have led them to *rethink* the brief—the mental model guiding the whole project. Only when they conducted some interviews themselves did they run into these surprising insights.

Immersion in a new social or geographical environment accelerates the development of mental models. For example, when researchers studied the origins of new products at the Norwegian telecom operator Telenor, they found that many of Telenor's product concepts came from people immersed in environments outside of the R&D department. One of its most successful services, a mobile payment system in Pakistan called "Easypaisa," originated from someone who was visiting the field. As the researchers noted, "We saw this in many of Telenor's ideas—they originate with people who work closely with the market."[6]

When choosing an environment to spend time in, we should think about colliding our idea with extreme environments: going to where the need for the new thing is the highest, or where the constraints are strongest. For example:

- The CEO of a confectionary company could spend time in environments around the world (cities, suburbs, villages) where chocolate sales have collapsed. He could mull over his ideas about the future direction of the company while observing the environments and kinds of people the company will have to win back to its business.

- An education company with a mission to reform schooling could send its head of product development to sit in on classes in a range of thriving and struggling schools around the country.

- The CEO of an industrial tools manufacturer could visit construction sites, having conversations with people on the ground about the pros and cons of her evolving mental model for 3D-printed, distributed manufacturing of tools.

- The chief technology officer of an airline might have an idea for improving the way its airport lounges operate. They could be sent to spend three days working in a variety of airport lounges, alternately doing normal work and stepping back to reflect on anything that arises relevant to their idea.

Probe

Another kind of action to collide mental models with reality is to shape or prod the world—creating something or trying it out—to provoke feedback and surprise.

PROBE EARLY

The concept of testing a product is familiar. But we should be probing the world long before we get to the point of having a minimally viable product, even before our idea is clear in our own mind. For the goal is not to test a developed idea yet, but to further prompt your own imagination. To return to the example of the car-sharing company Turo, founder Clark initially set out to do a pilot project before he realized there was something he could do right away:

> I was going out fundraising to try to do a pilot. And the feedback that I kept getting from investors was, "Cute idea, but nobody's going to drive my Range Rover." And so, what I did was I spent $1,000 to launch a really crappy website. At the time, there was no Squarespace or whatever. You actually had to pay an engineer to get a website up. And then, I printed out 10,000 postcards. And I went out onto street corner and handed them out . . . On this crappy website, there was a little form to sign up your car. It was completely unactionable. There were no next steps. But I got 40 people to sign up their cars. And so, this took us from a random, intangible idea to something very tangible.[7]

The value of doing this was to spur Clark's imagination, as well as that of investors. By getting out there early and probing the world (in this case, random passers-by), Clark kicked off a cycle of action and rethinking that drove the evolution of his counterfactual mental model.

The lesson from Clark is that we should act early. Rather than being held up by official processes and the expectations of others, figure out what you could do right now, or this week, to collide your emerging idea with the world.

PROBE SELECTIVELY

Another way to probe the world is to bring elements of your mental model to life selectively, either enacting it on a small scale or enacting one part of the model.

For instance, imagine you are the CEO of a real estate company and you want to reimagine your business. You have a tentative idea that real estate agents could become more like event planners for the entire experience of moving house: décor, logistics, and financial planning, in addition to the task of finding the right place. How can you collide this idea with the world? Organizing a large retraining and pilot program would take a long time and would not give you a chance to quickly create a mind-world reimagination loop. Instead, think smaller: contact one imaginative real estate agent in your company you know personally and get them to try out the idea for their next client, while you perhaps accompany them in the background.

While observing, you might think of new services to integrate, consider large-scale customer research you want to commission, or realize that acquiring a furniture moving company might be a way forward. The situation you are looking at is not statistically significant (one customer), but by acting out the imaginative idea in a microcosm, you bring to life some of its multiple interacting dimensions to feed your imagination.

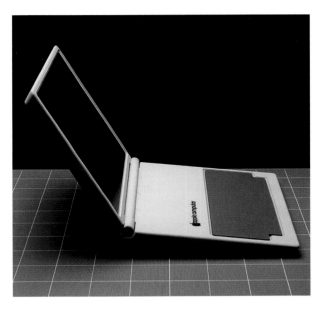

Figure 5-7 Nonfunctional Apple laptop shell from the 1980s

Source: Courtesy of frog design inc.

Another example of selective probing comes from the early days of Apple when the company contracted Hartmut Esslinger of frog design to create product prototypes. (See figure 5-7.)

For Apple, the core of its mental model around computers was how the object would look and feel—different from the industry's dominant mental model oriented around functionality. It wanted a computer to be valuable by being simple. And it wanted to differentiate from the competition not by foregrounding the technology, but presenting relatable

The Mathematics of Serendipity

The process of imagining, creating, and reimagining is somewhere between being completely random and completely controllable. It involves a lot of serendipity—a word coined in 1754 by British writer Horace Walpole, who wrote a story, "The Three Princes of Serendip" (a former name for Sri Lanka), the heroes of which "were always making discoveries, by accidents and sagacity, of things they were not in quest of."[a]

We know serendipity from experience. However, it also has an underlying mathematical structure. In research published in the journal *Nature*, the BCG Henderson Institute collaborated with the London Institute for Mathematical Sciences to model the search for valuable combinations of components at differing levels of complexity. For example, we modeled food recipes (varying in complexity, meaning the number of unique components) and ingredients (looking at the average complexity of the dishes they occur in).[b]

The gastronomy graph shows a range of ingredients ranked vertically by how often they occur in valid recipes. As you move from left to right, the size and complexity of the recipe set increases; oregano, for example, at the bottom, only occurs in more complex recipes. Bell peppers and vinegar are increasingly useful as the set of recipes becomes more complex, whereas cocoa and corn become less useful.

We did the same for software products and the tools used to make them. Google Analytics is near the top of the technology graph: it is part of most products. JavaScript is used with increasing frequency in more complex products.

When you are trying to bump into something new, it turns out that different ingredients will be more or less useful depending on the distribution of complexity of products in the space you are exploring. That is, if you are searching an area where not much has been invented, it pays to focus on simple ingredients to make simple new recipes. If you are searching a high-complexity space, where lots has been discovered already, it pays to try out complex recipes and to collect components that might be useful later. Hopefully, you stumble on the equivalent of vinegar, or JavaScript, which get more and more useful as you explore more complicated, nonobvious dishes or products.

When we are talking about mental models, *ideas* are components. For example, Shelby Clark of Turo had the idea of peer-to-peer marketplaces stuck in his head. This turned out to be a component like JavaScript: useful in many unpredictable—serendipitous—ways.

We can draw some key lessons from this for imagination. First, as we act in the world, we should expect and look out for serendipity—running into something valuable and novel—because it is a mathematical inevitability. Second, when there are a lot of easy wins in an unexplored area, we should focus on speed: building simple things and rapidly colliding them with the world. Third, most counterintuitively, when the wins are hard to find, it makes sense to collect and hold on to things that have rising utility with complexity, like the idea of peer-to-peer marketplaces, bell peppers, scallions, or JavaScript. In mature innovation spaces in big companies, when the dominant tone is serious, settled, and practical, we should actually seek *more* things that don't have an immediate use. We should be more like magpies, collecting shiny, interesting ideas, increasing the likelihood of unusual serendipitous combinations.

NOTES

a. *Oxford English Dictionary*, online edition, 2020.

b. T. M. A. Fink et al., "Serendipity and Strategy in Rapid Innovation," *Nature Communications* 8 (2017).

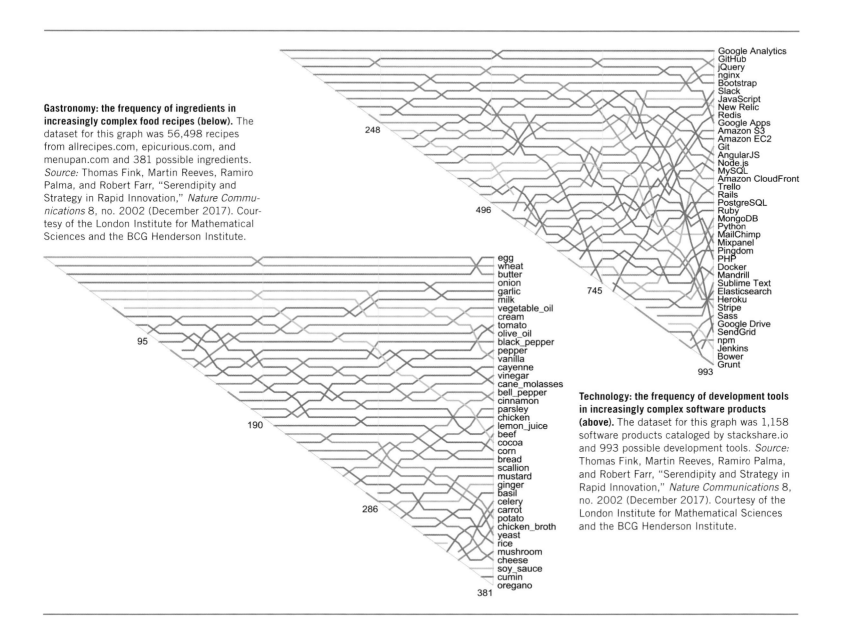

Gastronomy: the frequency of ingredients in increasingly complex food recipes (below). The dataset for this graph was 56,498 recipes from allrecipes.com, epicurious.com, and menupan.com and 381 possible ingredients. *Source:* Thomas Fink, Martin Reeves, Ramiro Palma, and Robert Farr, "Serendipity and Strategy in Rapid Innovation," *Nature Communications* 8, no. 2002 (December 2017). Courtesy of the London Institute for Mathematical Sciences and the BCG Henderson Institute.

Technology: the frequency of development tools in increasingly complex software products (above). The dataset for this graph was 1,158 software products cataloged by stackshare.io and 993 possible development tools. *Source:* Thomas Fink, Martin Reeves, Ramiro Palma, and Robert Farr, "Serendipity and Strategy in Rapid Innovation," *Nature Communications* 8, no. 2002 (December 2017). Courtesy of the London Institute for Mathematical Sciences and the BCG Henderson Institute.

objects. Later, Steve Jobs would articulate this mental model as the idea of a "friendly" computer.[8]

Producing a small, viable prototype laptop in the 1980s would have raised many engineering and manufacturing challenges. It would have been normal to try and solve these first. Instead, Apple began with the one thing it wanted to get right: whether it could make a laptop-like object that looked friendly. It could explore this early and comparatively cheaply by designing, creating, reimagining, and redesigning product shells.

In relation to your own idea, you can ask:

- Is there a way I can try this idea out in microcosm?

- Is there one critical feature, or even a side feature, of this mental model that I can try out now?

We should produce a representative sample, or a minimum viable product, when we want to persuade others, especially others who may be skeptical of our idea. The point of this exercise is not to persuade anyone, but to support our own rethinking loop.

PROBE PLAYFULLY

Another way of probing the world is to act playfully. In play, we are not aiming for a goal or testing a hypothesis. Rather, we have a starting point and improvise based on our imagination from there, driven by a sense of "why not?" (See the sidebar "The Function of Play.")

Play can help evolve mental models or reveal new models and paths to growth. For example, Play-Doh, originally

Aye, Alexander—but what is it?

I don't know yet, Mama. I'm trying to get the look and feel right first.

called Kutol Cleaner, began as a product to clean wallpaper, until business owner Joe McVicker overheard a teacher saying that kids in art class found modeling clay too tough to manipulate. On a whim, McVicker shipped a box of wallpaper cleaner to the school, and the class loved it.[9] We can suppose McVicker thought something like, "Why not? Might as well try it." He was acting playfully, improvising. He was then savvy enough to use the surprise result to fully reimagine his business. (See figure 5-8.)

We might feel that play doesn't, or shouldn't, happen much in business, except in companies probably much more fun than our own, like Play-Doh. However, the underlying mindset is valuable across all kinds of businesses and organizations.

The story of Google Maps also began with play. In 2004, then CEO of Google Eric Schmidt was in a meeting with his team. Cofounder Sergey Brin was also there but was not paying attention. Instead he was playing around on his laptop

Figure 5-8 Kutol Wall Cleaner was reimagined as Play-Doh

Source: Courtesy of Hasbro.

with a tool he had discovered, Keyhole, a browsable satellite map of the world. Brin searched for his own house and then looked up the houses of the people next to him in the meeting. As *Vox* reported:

> He'd shown his laptop to a couple people, and people said, "Oh shit, do me, do me." And this guy doing the presentation was really starting to sweat, and Sergey eventually gets up and unplugs the projector, says "This thing's cool and we should buy it," and he plugs his laptop into the projector and shows us Keyhole. And, literally, these executives are shouting out their addresses because they want to zoom in on their houses from space.[10]

Google eventually acquired Keyhole, which grew into Google Maps. The journey started, however, with putting the official goal of a meeting on hold to explore something in a playful way. They accelerated their imagination by messing around with something in the world.

PROBE ITERATIVELY

Another key to action that can accelerate imagination is to probe the world iteratively. Colliding a mental model with the world once is rarely enough; rather, you have to set up a dialogue between mind and reality. (See figure 5-9.)

Sometimes, probing iteratively can lead to a transformational surprise, as in Charles Goodyear's accidental invention of rubber for car tires:

> After learning about rubber, he convinced himself he could make his fortune by turning it into useful objects like waterproof shoes. All attempts ended in disaster and his life became a catalog of misery and misfortune. His shoes melted in the summer heat, six

The Function of Play

We don't usually think of play as being an essential part of business. Play, in a business context, looks like an optional extra: something you do after you've finished work, rather than an integral part of work itself. There are gestures toward playfulness in some modern offices: beanbags, LEGO corners, foosball tables, and so on. But these often just suggest that there are fun things you can theoretically do if you finish all your work and still want to stay in the office. They aren't often designed to make the work itself more imaginative and valuable.

What is play and why is it useful in business? Play is imagination-driven improvisation: it is a way of acting on imagination, which creates surprises that further inspire imagination.

The key to play is improvisation. As described by psychologist Mihály Csíkszentmihályi, play happens when we do things without much premeditation that are within our ability. For example, a pianist might play (in the playing around sense) by trying new chords and melodies as they come to her mind. She imagines something and then acts it out, without analysis or planning. The resulting unpredictable musical context she creates may inspire her to come up with further improvisational moves. We interviewed jazz musician Philip Clouts, who described this in his own work: "An idea for a piece will often come when I'm at the piano. When I'm playing around, something might come up and then I will pursue it because it seems interesting. You play around and you stumble across something. It's about being in the process of doing something musical, which leads to a musical idea, which might be strong enough to warrant working on."[a]

A basic condition for play is that the situation is derisked: there are no repercussions for doing something unexpected. This enables us to act unhindered by fear of consequences, simply driven by the imagination of the moment.

As Csíkszentmihályi writes, "Play is action generating action: a unified experience flowing from one moment to the next."[b] When things work well, play creates a mental state called "flow," "in which people are so involved in an activity that nothing else seems to matter," which is highly conductive to learning.[c]

We can describe the function of play, therefore, as derisked, accelerated learning. It is useful in business because it creates a fast feedback loop between mind and world. It is action that accelerates imagination. When we play, we let a half-formed, imaginative idea—which we might describe as a hunch—dictate our action. Free of potential judgment and the requirements of planning, we can quickly set up a back-and-forth with the world. Whether we are messing around with an interesting online tool we discovered, doing a minute-scale test of a product on a nonrepresentative sample, or printing postcards to hand out on the street, we are acting quickly to create a context in which we might be inspired to rethink further.

One example of useful play in business is the LEGO Serious Play Method, which is a facilitated meeting and problem-solving process in which participants construct models from building blocks and are prompted by a series of questions, probing deeper and deeper into the subject. Indeed, the name "LEGO" is an abbreviation of Danish words "LEg GOdt," meaning "play well." And the imagination games throughout this book are also designed to facilitate derisked, accelerated learning with colleagues around key capabilities of imagination.

NOTES

a. BCG Henderson Institute, interview with Philip Clouts, Axminster, England, June 17, 2019.

b. Mihály Csíkszentmihályi and Stith Bennett, "An Exploratory Model of Play," *American Anthropologist* 73, no. 1 (1971): 45–58.

c. Mihály Csíkszentmihályi, *Flow: The Psychology of Optimal Experience* (New York: Harper Perennial, 2008).

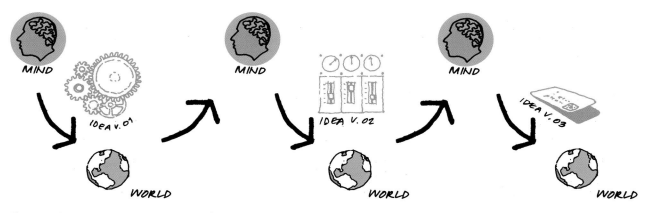

Figure 5-9 Ideas need to travel from mind to world and back repeatedly to develop

of his twelve children died in infancy, and his family had to live in grinding poverty . . . But Goodyear was determined. When debts landed him in jail, he simply asked his wife to bring him a rolling pin and some rubber and he carried on inventing in his cell. He finally made his big breakthrough when he accidentally dropped a piece of rubber on a hot stove. It cooked and shriveled into a hard black mass that Goodyear immediately spotted as the thing he'd wanted all along. This is how he developed the tough black rubber we use in tires today by a cooking process now known as vulcanization.[11]

Over multiple iterations, we give ourselves a chance to create as many interesting accidents and anomalies as possible. And in iterating, we don't just evolve the specific idea; we evolve the mind that is evolving the idea. If the iteration continues

over time, we can change many minds and eventually the whole company.

We can see this in the history of the LEGO Group, which began doing carpentry for local houses and churches, but has evolved over time in ways that could not have been predicted. (See figure 5-10.)

It can be surprisingly hard, on an emotional level, to let evolution beat design. It is difficult to let your favorite ideas change. Yet imagination when combined with iterated action can start us on a journey that leads to valuable things that we never expected.

Artist Jane South of the Pratt Institute shares her experience guiding people through the process of imagining, creating, and reimagining:

A sculpture student shows me a drawing and says, "This is what I am going to make." I say, "All right,

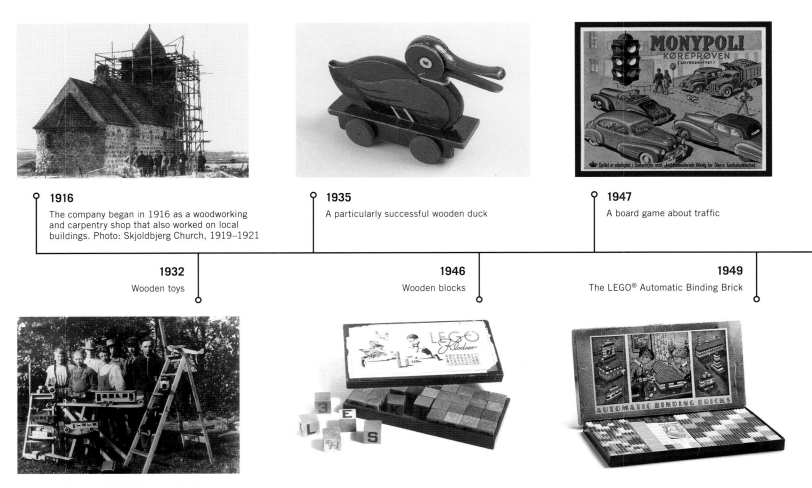

1916
The company began in 1916 as a woodworking and carpentry shop that also worked on local buildings. Photo: Skjoldbjerg Church, 1919–1921

1935
A particularly successful wooden duck

1947
A board game about traffic

1932
Wooden toys

1946
Wooden blocks

1949
The LEGO® Automatic Binding Brick

Figure 5-10 The LEGO® Group timeline

Source: © 2020 The LEGO Group, except wooden blocks, © Niels Aage Skovbo/Fokus Foto; Monypoli board game, LEGO AS, Denmark, 1947 via Creative Commons; *The LEGO Movie* poster, courtesy of AA Film Archive/Alamy Stock Photo; and *The LEGO Movie 2: The Second Part* poster, courtesy of BFA/Alamy Stock Photo.

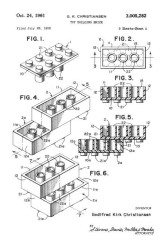

1958

The unique stud-and-tube system that lay the groundwork for the LEGO® System

1974

The LEGO® building figure

2003

LEGO® Serious Play® for business

1968

Expansion into parks: LEGOLAND®

1993

The LEGO® System: multiple themes, all intercompatible

2014 and 2019

LEGO® movies

Oh—that's Henry. He's trying to evolve.

go ahead." Next week I come back and what they've made looks nothing like their original drawing. Disappointed, the student says, "Oh my God, I've failed! I did not mean to make this . . ." Yet this is the point at which they are actually *creating* something. If an artist is determined to stick to their first idea, they miss all the opportunities for the imagination to allow other things they have encountered (all of those experiences recorded somewhere in your being) into play with whatever their initial impetus was. If the process of making is not surprising, it is not creative! It's not until you actually start *making*, that you open the door to this, and things manifest in a way you can't predict.[12]

What Blocks Action?

Some key pathologies stop ideas moving from mind to world and back again.

Ignoring Surprise

This block is the tendency in business to focus only on whether some initiative was successful according to predefined metrics such as customer satisfaction or revenue potential. We take an idea from the mind into the world, but not back into the mind for further evolution. The solution is for every formal and informal report on action to include what we learned in addition to any conclusions about success or failure.

Not Iterating

This is the block of giving an idea only one chance to evolve, which comes from thinking that the first iteration of the idea basically captures the value there is to be captured, rather than seeing the first iteration as a starting point for many cycles of reimagination.

The name of the rust-prevention spray WD-40 stands for "Water Displacement perfected on the 40th try" because it took the company forty attempts to get the formula right.[13] Yet the iteration was worth it because what started as a niche product in the aerospace industry in 1953 became hugely popular with home consumers. The solution, then, is to remember WD-40 as a symbolic product around imagination: a reminder that a starting idea will go through the reimagination loop perhaps forty times.

Reliance on Permission

This pathology is the often-pervasive sense, particularly in large businesses, that nothing can be done without permission from someone else. Similar to the mindset dominant during feudal times, this block derives from a fear of judgment by superiors. The mindset can persist even as one rises up the ranks, however, and even someone running a company can be held back by an ingrained feeling that they need some kind of permission—from the board, peers, or a comprehensive, unquestionable feasibility study—before acting on an idea. The solution is to remember that permission makes less and less sense the closer you come to the position of leader.

Overemphasis on Analysis and Deduction

This pathology is the expectation that early-stage ideas should be backed by as much analysis as further developed ideas. In reality this expectation means that everyone must hide how they *actually* explore ideas in the early stages (when detailed analysis is impossible because they are still exploring what the idea is) or more often than not, avoid altogether the messy, unpredictable, and iterative process of developing new ideas. People still get inspiration from accidents, anomalies, and analogies and think of new mental models, but never act on them because the hurdles of required proof are too high and come too soon. In the next chapter, we look in more detail at less-specific metrics to apply the early stages of an idea. Detailed metrics should apply eventually, but the antidote to the overemphasis on analysis is to accept the messy, nonmeasurable early period of imagination.

Not Letting Go

This is the pathology of holding on to treasured ideas and mental models, rather than letting them evolve. The opposite of this is an important virtue: the mental habit of holding lightly onto one's own ideas. We can take inspiration here from science, which cultivates a willingness to move on from an initial idea when it is falsified or when a more comprehensive or insightful mental model is presented. Biologist Richard Dawkins explains:

> I have previously told the story of a respected elder statesman of the Zoology Department at Oxford when I was an undergraduate. For years he had passionately believed, and taught, that the Golgi Apparatus (a microscopic feature of the interior of cells) was not real . . . Every Monday afternoon it was the custom for the whole department to listen to a research talk by a visiting lecturer. One Monday, the visitor was an American cell biologist who presented completely convincing evidence that the Golgi Apparatus was real. At the end of the lecture, the old man strode to the front of the hall, shook the American by the hand and said—with passion—"My dear fellow, I wish to thank you. I have been wrong these fifteen years."[14]

Games to Play

To practice some of the techniques in this chapter, you can play some imagination-provoking games with colleagues.

The News Headlines Game

This game centers around the idea of being monomaniacal about a new, imaginative mental model. Choose an idea you have been thinking about recently. Go to your favorite news site, and for every news story on the home page, try to see your idea in it. Ask yourself:

- What is one way I can connect this story to my idea? Feel free to be playful.

- What do I notice about this story when I read it with my idea in mind?

Next, reflect and consider if any of these encounters of your idea with the world raised any interesting or surprising thoughts about your idea. See if this suggests any ways to build on, deepen, or refine your counterfactual mental model. Do this for a week to explore the full potential of your idea across a range of contexts.

The $100 Game

Pick one idea you want to collide with the world. Then think of:

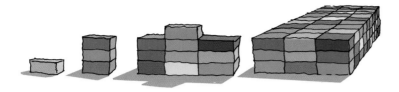

- One way you could act on it, given $100,000 and three months

- How you could act on it with $10,000 and one month

- How you could act on it with $100 and one week

- One cheap, easy, perhaps playful way you could probe the world around this idea *today*, using the resources you have right now

Then swap ideas with a colleague: listen to their idea and explain yours to them. Answer the same set of questions for their idea, then discuss the suggestions you came up with for each other's ideas. If you feel moved, do the action you came up with before the end of the day.

Good Questions to Ask

Some good questions to ask to learn and enrich your idea through colliding it with reality are:

- Where do I want to focus my attention to move the idea forward?

- What is one area of knowledge I could dive into to feed my imagination around the idea?

- What would be the ideal environment to observe the need for this idea?

- What is one dimension of the idea that I could explore immediately and at minimal cost?

- How could I *play* with the idea?

Organizational Diagnostic

We can assess how good our organization is at supporting the task explored in this chapter: colliding ideas with the world to accelerate imagination. Each question is linked to a related action in the chapter, which could be a useful starting point if your organization scores poorly on that question.

	Related action	Never	Rarely or less than once a year	Sometimes or once a month to once a year	Usually or once a week to once a month	Always or more often than weekly
		(1)	(2)	(3)	(4)	(5)
Employees talk to each other often about speculative and early-stage ideas.	Be monomaniacal					
Employees visit new geographical or social environments to develop new ideas.	Visit a relevant environment					
Our firm encourages and invests resources in developing an employee's own early-stage ideas.	Create a learning journey					
Our firm tries early-stage ideas without expecting them (at first) to be justified by financial analysis.	Probe early					
People in our firm can generally ask forgiveness rather than permission when trying new things.	Probe playfully					
Employees have playful conversations at work.	Probe playfully					
People with ideas in our company are willing to try them out in a rough form and get real-world feedback.	Probe iteratively					
Our company reports on lessons learned from initiatives as well as direct financial outcomes.	Probe iteratively					
TOTAL						

After you have added up your total, score your current situation: 31–35, excellent; 21–30, good; 11–20, moderate; 0–10, poor. To benchmark your score against other organizations, please visit www.theimaginationmachine.org.

Chapter Six

THE EPIDEMIC

Recruit Holdings, owner of Indeed and Glassdoor, has $23 billion of revenue across businesses in HR, education, and marketing. Yet even at this scale, the company is able to identify imaginative ideas from its employees and spread those ideas to inspire collective exploration by new teams, resulting in profitable new businesses. As Takanori Makiguchi, executive manager of Recruit's Management Competence Research Institute, said to us: "Recruit needs to change constantly. This means changing minds."[1]

An example of one person's idea being amplified to inspire others is the story of Fumihiro Yamaguchi. In 2010, Yamaguchi was a middle manager in Recruit's education division. While doing customer research, he noticed there were lots of one-on-one tutoring services and lectures to help students with exam preparation, but no scalable online service. He imagined something to fill this gap, and his manager encouraged him to share his idea at Recruit's annual ideas contest, Ring. With no approval process, any employee can submit an idea to the contest. When Yamaguchi

shared his idea, people came forward to form a team with him. Every year, Recruit staff form almost a thousand such ad hoc employee teams, an achievement highlighted in its annual report.[2]

After passing an initial screening, Yamaguchi received a research budget. His team tried things out, reimagined, and received further funds. Eventually they received $18 million to launch the service as a subsidiary business within Recruit.[3] The result, StudySapuri, now has 1.4 million paid subscribers and, together with other online service businesses, including others that grew out of Ring, generates $748 million revenue at 15 percent annual growth.[4] Ring has also produced a beauty salon platform, Hot Pepper, and wedding planning platform, Zexy. All these businesses were once no more than ideas in the minds of employees, which in most companies would probably have gone nowhere as people put aside their speculations to get on with assigned work. (See figure 6-1.)

• • •

Chapter Overview

The problem of intersubjectivity

How can we collectively imagine?

TALK TOGETHER

- Name things
- Train for storytelling
- Train for listening
- Support brokers

FOCUS TOGETHER

- Use collective play
- Run a festival

MOVE TOGETHER

- Relocate and colocate

PROBE TOGETHER

- Distribute autonomy
- Suspend precision

Blocks to collective imagination

EXCESSIVE COMPLIANCE

CACOPHONY

SILOS

DEPERSONALIZATION

Games to play

THE MESSY FOUNDATIONS GAME

THE NAMING GAME

Good questions to ask

Organizational diagnostic

Figure 6-1 Employee sharing ideas at Recruit Holdings
Source: Courtesy of Recruit Holdings.

For an idea to move beyond being an individual's pet project, it needs others to adopt it. Like a virus, it needs to spread from one person to many. So how does a new mental model spread from one brain to inspire and enlist the imaginations of others? How do we move from individual to collective imagination?

This chapter shifts focus from harnessing individual imagination to looking at things you can do at a collective level to harness imagination across your business. We examine the challenge of "intersubjectivity," ways to create collective imagination, common blocks to achieving this, games to play, questions to ask, and an organizational diagnostic.

The Problem of Intersubjectivity

When we spread a developing mental model from one brain to others across a business, we amplify it in two ways. We accelerate its evolution, by driving collective reimagination. And we create social validation as people accept and engage with the idea until it becomes part of their work or lives.

A central challenge in spreading an idea, however, is the problem of intersubjectivity. How do you get multiple minds to work together on an intangible mental model of something that doesn't yet exist? We spoke to Swiss philosopher Eduard Marbach, who described the problem:

> From a Husserlian perspective, collective imagination is a really complex thing because it involves the challenge of intersubjectivity. How can two private mental worlds align to work together on the same mental "object"? This is less of a problem when you're dealing with things that already exist. If you show something in the real world to your neighbor, you can point to it and say, "Let's talk about that." But if you are in the middle of imagining something, it doesn't yet exist. Especially if you want to share imagination with someone while the idea is still nascent and amorphous. If you imagine something, and you want to have someone else with you, thinking about the same thing, you have to find some way to specify what you want to talk about.[5]

Figure 6-2 The Romantic movement emphasized the individual hero above the world: imagination as subjectivity rather than intersubjectivity

Source: Caspar David Friedrich (1774–1840), *Wanderer above the Sea of Fog*, circa 1817. © bpk Bildagentur/Hamburger Kunsthalle, Hamburg, Germany/ Elke Walford/Art Resource, NY.

The Romantic movement, which greatly shaped the popular understanding of imagination, also emphasized the challenge of intersubjectivity. Yet Romantics usually took this as a reason *not* to work with others. They often depicted the artist or inventor as a lone hero, rather than a hero in a collective or corporate context. (See figure 6-2.)

If we can solve the intersubjectivity challenge, we create collective imagination: multiple minds working together on

Figure 6-3 Actions to create collective imagination

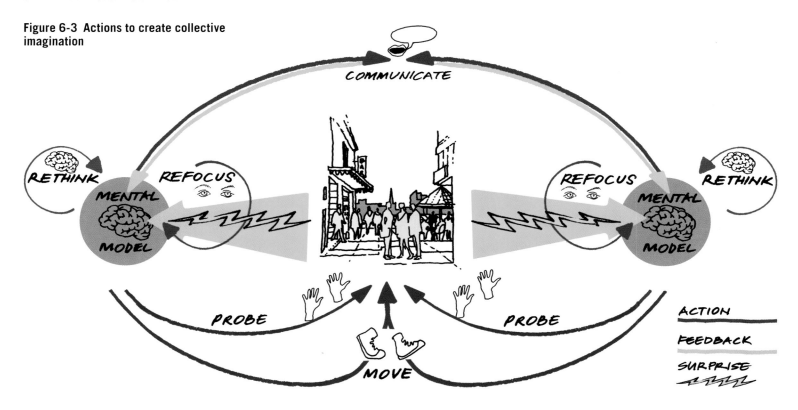

the same evolving mental model, creating momentum toward fully realizing an idea.

How Can We Collectively Imagine?

To overcome the intersubjectivity problem, we can't simply plug our brains together. Our output needs to become the surprising input to someone else's brain to prompt their imagination. The chief action to achieve this is obviously communication, but we can also use the actions explored in the previous chapter, but at the collective level: focus together, move together, and probe the world together (see figure 6-3).

In what follows we explore each of these actions, looking at specific moves we can make to help ideas move from the

COLLECTIVE IMAGINATION

individual to the collective level—to progress from an initial, subjective idea to synchronized exploration based on a shared mental model.

Talk Together

NAME THINGS

One way to communicate a new mental model is to give it a name. The importance of language, specifically naming, is easy to underestimate because we are so familiar with the named creations around us: fridge, restaurant, smartphone. It is easy to forget how strange these things were when they were just unlabeled thoughts.

Fundamentally, a name delimits something new, allowing us to refer to a shared object. A name makes an intersubjective thing out of what was once just an idea in one person's mind. Shakespeare articulated this in memorable lines:

> *And as imagination bodies forth*
> *The forms of things unknown, the poet's pen*
> *Turns them to shapes, and gives to airy nothing*
> *A local habitation and a name.*

On top of the fundamental task of creating a label, there are three additional jobs a name can do, which may not be initially obvious: help people feel familiar with the unfamiliar, signal how something will be used, and draw attention to something (see figure 6-4).

Even though an Apple Watch is actually a sensor and computer on your wrist, a watch is what people already know, so the name works by taking people to a familiar starting point. In contrast, in 1905, no one knew what a vacuum cleaner was. So we got Griffith's Improved Vacuum Apparatus for Removing Dust from Carpets, a name that carefully explains the function.[6] In contrast again, everyone knows what T-shirts and pants are, to the point that we may have no interest in looking at another instance. In this case the principal challenge is drawing attention, so you end up applying a name like the brand FCUK.

LOOK!

A THING

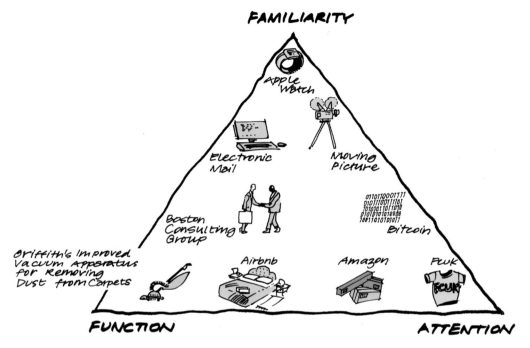

Figure 6-4 Jobs done by a name

Businesses, however, often waste the power to create new language. Effort is focused on giving catchy names to ordinary things, aiming for differentiation through language alone. As well as outlandish product names, this bias can cause us to unnecessarily rename ordinary words, like "leverage" for "use," or "learnings" for "lesson." A better strategy would be to only coin names for genuinely new, imaginative ideas as they arise in the business, and to be clear about the job to be done by those names.

It may be tempting when thinking imaginatively to look for a "creative" name, in the sense of an unfamiliar one. But the job of naming imaginative ideas is mostly about showing where something unusual fits in relation to what is familiar to us and indicating how something works. The mental model is already unfamiliar enough; the name should be the bridge between the counterfactual and quotidian worlds. The name FCUK only works because no one is confused about what a T-shirt is. When you have something revolutionary, an unrevolutionary name like Apple Watch or the Wright Flyer (which the Wright

FKUQ

A bad name for a vacuum cleaner in 1905, when no one had ever seen one before

brothers called their flying machine) is best. This is held up by research in linguistics, which shows the primary factor driving the adoption of neologisms is the familiarity of the linguistic parts.[7]

For example, let's say you are reforming the business to introduce more time for reflection. You could crystallize this idea, making it powerful and communicable, by giving it a function-oriented name: "The 10% Thinking Rule" or "The Reflective Company." Or suppose an employee suggests the idea of bringing cafés into retail banks. A manager could help spread this idea by naming it the "Café Bank," a name that's useful because it draws on two familiar mental models.

Looking at early mentions of now-familiar things, successful names for imaginative creations often start out as basic words trying simply to capture what the newfangled concept is about:[8]

Apple said that new applications for the iPhone could be purchased through the App Store, a new application that will let users download the applications directly to their devices.　　　*—Network World*, 2008

Depositors seal their deposits in envelopes which are provided and insert them in the "automatic teller," which flashes a Thank You sign and issues a receipt.　　　*—American Banker*, 1971

Postmaster General Summerfield plans split-second electronic mail.　　　*—Appleton Post-Crescent,* 1959

We were all photographed by the new cinematograph process, which makes moving pictures by winding off a reel of films.

　　　—Queen Victoria, in her journal, 1896

Associations with limited liability are of two kinds: in one, the liability of all partners is limited, in the other that of some of them only.　　　*—John Stuart Mill, 1848*

TRAIN FOR STORYTELLING

Many businesses train for communication skills but don't often focus on the skills needed specifically to communicate ideas about not-yet-existent things. Because the counterfactual, imagined model doesn't fully exist, it needs embodying in some other way to inspire others. This is where stories can be powerful.

It's the Wright Flyer I. The next one we thought could be called the Wright Flyer II.

Simply passing information to someone is not enough, since (1) if there is no interest nothing is achieved, (2) we are swimming in information and information alone doesn't automatically create interest, and (3) we need to be selective because we can't tell it all. As Nietzsche said, "It is not enough to prove something, one has to seduce or elevate people to it."[9]

What's actually going on when we share an idea? We are not, in fact, *passing* an object from one brain to another. We are *provoking* another brain, hoping the person becomes inspired enough to imagine something similar to what we are imagining. Often, this does not work. You try to explain your idea, and the other person imagines something different and uninteresting. In your subjective world, the mental model is an exciting and beautiful castle. When you talk to other people, they might create the equivalent of a dingy studio apartment in their mind's eye.

Techniques for storytelling can help bridge this inter-subjective gap because stories evoke and energize: they get people to see what you see as well as motivate them to care.

For example, in 1949, Charles Merrill had developed a mental model for the transformation of his bank. He now faced the social challenge of inducing the firm's partners to share in the development and application of his vision. He did this effectively through storytelling. For example, he talked about stock-buying workshops they had run for women in San Francisco, framing these, in his final sentence, as part of a grand mission to realize the full potential of a new model of brokerage.

> It has astonished us, I admit, to have so many women saying, "Information, Please," on the subject of stocks and bonds . . . There was another highly satisfying development, too. Some of the women asked if we would give courses for their husbands. This meant that our merchandise was beginning to be discussed in a few homes where it had never been discussed before. It is a small step, admittedly, when you consider that only about 7% of the 52,000,000 families in this country own any common or preferred stock at all.
>
> We do not know accurately, of course, how many of the remaining 93% have available funds for investment in our country's industries, but we do know that there are tens of millions who could buy our products but

Our imaginative mental model (left) vs. what this creates in someone else's mind (right). *Source:* (left) tucko019/ iStock by Getty Images and (right) Justin Masterson via Creative Commons.

do not. That is why there is no more challenging and necessary mass merchandising project than that which faces investment houses today.[10]

According to the *Oxford English Dictionary*, a story is "an oral or written narrative account of events." This contrasts with an argument or a set of data, although both of these can be incorporated into stories, as Merrill does. Stories are effective because they engage more of our minds than merely the capacity for explicit reasoning. A good story enables two brains to experience one thing, known in cognitive science as "brain coupling." Neuroscientist Uri Hasson has studied this phenomenon, showing that both the receivers and tellers of a story share similar brain activity while the story is being told.[11]

We can identify some techniques of effective storytelling, which can be used in enlisting others to help evolve and amplify new ideas:

- Use emotional content; for example, Merrill talks about being "astonished."

- Play to many senses; for example images, video, evocative description.

Like our brochure says: light, airy, mountain views! A beautiful place to start a family . . .

- Use specific color and detail rather than generalizations or summaries.

- Incorporate the structure of an archetypal narrative, if possible (see the sidebar "Archetypal Narratives").

TRAIN FOR LISTENING

As well as being good storytellers, people need to be good *receivers* of early-stage ideas. Listening is a skill: how to be imaginatively generous as a listener, rather than impatient and dismissive.

Like the need for storytelling, the need for good listening comes from the fact that imaginative ideas often don't communicate easily. New mental models go through stages of vagueness and incoherency where the value is not at all

obvious. Jony Ive, the head designer at Apple for twenty-six years, describes the origins of the App Store:

> And so, as the potential for a vast range of apps became clear, so did the idea for an App Store. But it's important to remember . . . the actual value of the idea, certainly at the beginning, was rather vague and it was nebulous and it was very difficult to articulate. We made some prototypes and the early prototypes really described more of the problems than the opportunities. The early prototypes and the actions of the resolving technology were exceptionally crude, but they were made to explore the idea, and not to justify it. Now, these ideas, they weren't vulnerable or fragile for a couple of weeks or for a couple of months, these ideas were fragile for years.[12]

Ive's design team solved the intersubjectivity problem: "fragile" and "rather vague" mental models could come to live in the imaginations of others. This was possible because the design team members were imaginative listeners; they could pick up on whatever starting point the other person was offering and run with it in their own imaginations. For example, the development of the iMac began with an unusual, half-formed mental model from designer Doug Satzger. He suggested the team make something "like an egg."[13]

In most business contexts, this suggestion would be too weird to lead anywhere. Imagine the conversation between the chief technology officer (CTO) and a vice president (VP) in your company:

Archetypal Narratives

Anthropologists and psychologists have identified several archetypal patterns in stories across human cultures.[a] There are some core features of powerful stories:

- A protagonist or group of protagonists

- A trigger that sets the protagonist off on some kind of journey or struggle

- A struggle, usually including confusion, failed attempts, antagonists, and mentors

- A resolution, or vision of a resolution ahead

One lesson for business leaders is that protagonists are important. The originators and early developers of an imaginative mental model are a vital part of the story that helps that model spread. Often in business, an idea is divorced from its protagonists; it is passed on to managers, written up in a depersonalized way, and sent to people who have no connection with the original context. Recruit Holdings has a different approach: it encourages the originator to see themselves as an entrepreneurial hero by letting them build their own team and champion their own idea. The mental model thus stays linked to the personal story, which gives it more evocative power in the minds of others. In other words, Recruit deliberately creates heroes.

To become a great storyteller, you should gain familiarity with great stories, not necessarily to quote them directly, but to hone your instincts for description, language choice, and use of mental imagery. Great speech givers through history— Martin Luther King Jr., Charles de Gaulle, Sojourner Truth, Mary Wollstonecraft, Pericles—were all familiar with great stories, which seeped into their way of communicating.

For inspiration, here is a selection of works across art forms organized by the seven basic plots found throughout human storytelling:[b]

Voyage and return: The protagonist leaves the familiar and ventures into a geographically or socially distant place. They return with experience, although the insights they bring are often not accepted by their old friends. Examples: *The Myth of Orpheus*, *The Time Machine*, *The Republic*, *Brideshead Revisited*, *Journey to the West* (西遊記), *Wilhelm Meister's Apprenticeship*

Escape from death: The protagonist sets out to defeat a dangerous or disruptive force that threatens themselves or their group, often transforming themselves or their group in the process. Examples: *Popol Vuh*, *The Myth of Perseus*, *Star Wars: A New Hope*, *Ramayana* (रामायणम्), *Beowulf*, *The Táin* (*Táin Bó Cúailnge*), *Harry Potter and the Deathly Hallows*

Rags to riches: The protagonist starts off marginalized or dejected before discovering and using their true strengths, gaining influence, wealth, or success in some other form. Examples: *The Ugly Duckling*, *The Benny Goodman Story*, *Jane Eyre*, *Great Expectations*, *The Red and the Black*, *Siddhartha*

The quest: The protagonist has a clear task to accomplish or location to reach. They face setbacks and doubts, and must grow internally to accomplish the goal. Examples: *The Myth of Bayajidda*, *Apocalypse*

Now, The Aeneid, The Odyssey, The Lord of the Rings, The Divine Comedy, Treasure Island

Comedy: The protagonist is lost in chaos through confusion of identities and misunderstandings. Everything gets tied in knots until, through genius or accident, the knot is untied and order is restored. Examples: *The Clouds; A Night in Casablanca; A Midsummer Night's*

Ah, yes! You are clearly stuck in an archetypal narrative.

Dream; Three Men in a Boat; Lock, Stock and Two Smoking Barrels

Tragedy: The protagonist is sucked into a downward spiral, resolved in destruction, although the destruction might be a necessary loss, in which case the story ends in solemn rejoicing. Examples: *King Lear, Citizen Kane, To Have and Have Not, The Myth of Icarus, Anna Karenina, Dream of the Red Chamber* (紅樓夢), *One Hundred Years of Solitude*

Rebirth: The protagonist falls into a frozen condition; they are physically or spiritually stuck, trying to rediscover life and vigor. An act of redemption or unlocking occurs and their vitality is restored. Examples: *Groundhog Day, The Myth of Osiris, Crime and Punishment, The Secret Garden*

NOTES

a. Christopher Booker, *The Seven Basic Plots: Why We Tell Stories* (New York: Continuum, 2004).

b. Ibid.

CTO: What are you thinking for our next hit product?

VP: I've been considering eggs—how simple an egg is. I haven't really got any further with this yet. But I am hopeful.

Happily, the Apple design team listened to Satzger's egg suggestion and was inspired to head down the road that led to the iMac. As Ive describes the underlying dynamics: "We have so much trust as a team that we don't censor our ideas because we are nervous and scared that they will sound absurd . . . A lot of this process is about listening."[14]

This ability to share an early-stage idea without being harshly judged is something that should not be limited to design teams. For ideas to spread in a business, we need to cultivate the skill of imaginative listening, the skill of finding triggers for inspiration, rather than targets for criticism, in what the other person is saying. When someone is listening with imaginative generosity, they might ask themselves: "What if what this person is saying *could* really be revolutionary?" "What might an egg-inspired computer be like?" "What does this odd fragment of a suggestion lead me to rethink?"

Finding inspiration in what the other person is saying is helped by a number of supporting skills: tolerance of ambiguity; openness to going in a direction you hadn't thought about; suspension of judgment; and encouragement and patience as a default—based on hope that there are good things to be found together, even if they are not immediately obvious.

Across a business, some actions to train for and cultivate these skills are:

- Edit hiring and promotion criteria to identify people who have proven themselves good at imaginative listening.

- Include a focus on this skill in training programs, especially in relation to building and managing teams.

- Advocate for the importance of imaginative listening via your own communications and at company events.

SUPPORT BROKERS

In supporting the spread of imaginative ideas, of key value are those employees who can talk to other people across the varied communities and tribes within a business. We can picture an organization like an archipelago. There are islands of strongly connected people, separated by gaps (see figure 6-5).

Within a network, we can roughly divide individuals into two kinds: brokers and insiders. Insiders stay on an island, with the team they know. Brokers connect the islands; they create bridges of intersubjectivity between groups.[15]

Tim O'Reilly, an influential thinker in Silicon Valley who coined the term "Web 2.0," is a prime example of a broker, engaging with a diverse network. He describes one of his projects, which involved talking to former CEO of Google Eric Schmidt:

> I was working on what we called the Gov 2.0 Summit, which brought together people from Silicon Valley with people from government, and led to my formulation of "government as a platform." When I began working on the event, I talked to Eric Schmidt because I knew he'd been doing a bunch of work in Washington. And he said, "Tim, just go talk to a lot of people and then you'll make sense of it. That's what you do."[16]

O'Reilly's way of operating is the opposite of what usually happens in a business, where we are more likely to talk with our immediate team than to "go talk to a lot of people."

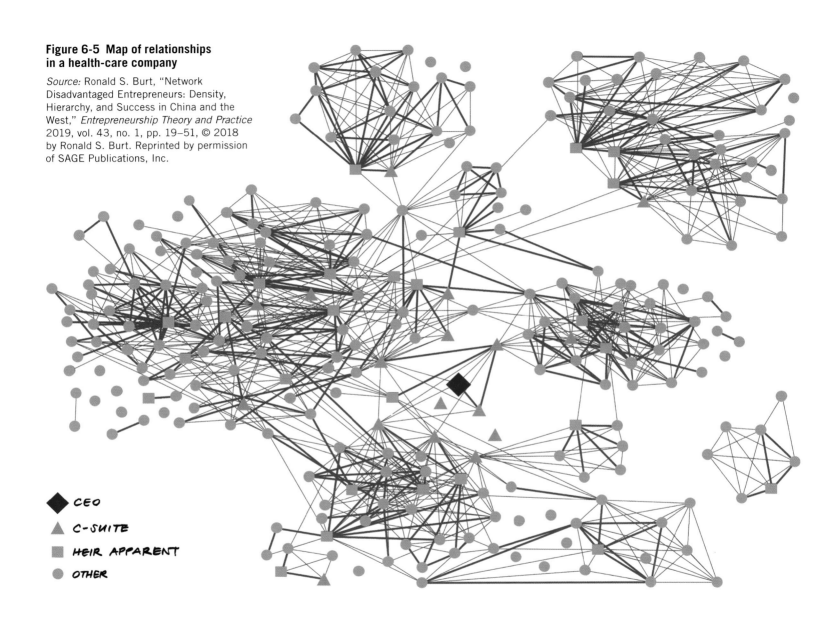

Figure 6-5 Map of relationships in a health-care company

Source: Ronald S. Burt, "Network Disadvantaged Entrepreneurs: Density, Hierarchy, and Success in China and the West," *Entrepreneurship Theory and Practice* 2019, vol. 43, no. 1, pp. 19–51, © 2018 by Ronald S. Burt. Reprinted by permission of SAGE Publications, Inc.

◆ CEO

▲ C-SUITE

■ HEIR APPARENT

● OTHER

Insiders who know one island well and operate effectively on it are important. But a company needs brokers as well, who work across and beyond the firm. Sociologist Ron Burt refers to the "import-export nature of brokerage-based creativity." That is, brokers help ideas spread and evolve by translating them from one group's mental models into another, creating new possibilities for surprise and rethinking. "An idea mundane in one group can be a valuable insight in another."[17]

Brokers fulfill a crucial function, which is to help spread ideas through a diverse set of minds. This accelerates the mental model's evolution, as it spreads through a value chain of personalities with different experience and stocks of mental models, each of which bring different mental construction materials to the developing model.

Focus Together

USE COLLECTIVE PLAY

In addition to talking, another area of action that spreads ideas is mutual refocusing of attention. If two or more people can orient their attention to the same thing, that is a way of developing a shared understanding, bridging the intersubjectivity gap. A key activity in which this happens is collective play.

A landmark investigation of play, the book *Homo Ludens*, notes that all cultures set aside special zones for play: "The arena, the card-table, the magic circle, the temple, the stage, the screen, the tennis court, etc., are all in form and function play-grounds, isolated, hedged round, hallowed, within which special rules obtain."[18] Because play is set apart from normal goal-directed work, it can help to use physical space as a marker for different mental space. Media entrepreneur John Battelle describes a room he built to host musical improvising, which turned into a spot to play with business ideas (see figure 6-6):

> The room has whiteboards everywhere and a big bar, and all these instruments. My friend came over after I built it and he was like, "Oh my god this is awesome, I'm never leaving." So we started just very poorly playing music in that room. After about two months we had three others join us.
>
> What happened that I didn't expect, is that the whiteboards started filling up. Everybody in the band was a leader of some kind of business. My friend had a startup in health tech, one guy ran a physical storage company, another guy had an executive recruiting company. The band room became a place where we could jam not just on music but on *ideas*. The whiteboard would fill up with this crazy stuff. Then people

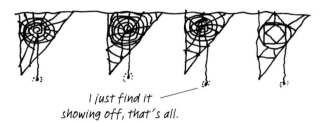

I just find it showing off, that's all.

. . . And I call this my ideas room.

Figure 6-6 John Battelle's room for improvisation—with music and ideas

Source: Courtesy of John Battelle.

started hearing about it and they asked if they could come do sessions in the band room. People with new ideas—tons of entrepreneurs came with new ideas, who just wanted to jam on them.[19]

The room was a place for people to bring imaginative mental models and focus collective attention on them. We can create spaces with a similar underlying principle. We don't have to use the clichéd setup of bean bags and colorful furniture. There are many ways to mark the space as different from the day-to-day: the lighting could be dimmer or there could be shelves of interesting books or a signal jammer to stop everyone's phones working to focus them on each other and leave behind the demands of the day.

Once you have a good space, as Battelle notes, "You have to know how to have a really interesting, intelligent, agile conversation."[20] The philosopher Aristotle systematized some advice around this. He observed that there are two bad extremes in discussions: being too serious and dull, and being too frivolous—which is dull in its own way. In between these two lies a mental quality Aristotle called *eutrapelia*, or "good-turning": being able to change direction playfully from serious to fun and back, engaging others in a rich but also light-hearted discussion.[21] Somewhere between the tedium and buffoonery lies inspiration, where sparks of thought arise in ourselves, to surprise and inspire others and vice versa.

RUN A FESTIVAL

Festivals can be another great way of synchronizing attention, celebrating and recognizing idea development, and spreading ideas. This doesn't happen often: most company meetings are taken up with reporting on goals, actions, and outcomes. In the BCG Henderson Institute's cross-industry survey, 55 percent of leaders said their company had no effective mechanisms for sharing and inspiring others with new and stimulating ideas.[22]

Recruit Holdings has developed a successful model: running two annual events, Ring and FORUM, which host short presentations on new business ideas and imaginative improvements to ways of working, in front of over one thousand staff members (see figure 6-7). The ideas are not presented as signed-off ventures but as works in progress; Recruit suggests employees "share 'story,' 'know-how,' and 'stance,' not only 'results.'"

Such in-person forums may be bad from the perspective of containing a viral pandemic, but they are powerful from the perspective of spreading ideas. Of course, we should only run in-person events when safe to do so (Recruit's 2020 event was online). But our techniques for amplifying ideas are the inverse of the social distancing measures used to contain Covid-19. The Recruit festival is a deliberate super-spreader event, in a good way.

Such events are effective in not just transmitting developing ideas but also motivating new journeys of imagination. Recruit surveyed a thousand employees across a range of companies about what affects intrinsic motivation, and having such festi-

Figure 6-7 Annual ideas FORUM at Recruit Holdings

Source: Courtesy of Recruit Holdings.

vals where employees gather to share ideas was one of the top five factors.* Festivals draw on people's natural desire for status to amplify counterfactual ideas: the attention of a large crowd creates excitement and a heroic status that rubs off on presenters. Recruit emphasizes this, drawing on marketing tools to create companywide "entrepreneur heroes."

---

* The others were the idea that the company belongs to the employee; giving authority to employees as a chance to grow; feeling free to ask colleagues for advice; and top management being close to employees.

Umwelts *and* Umgebungs

How do the people in a business collectively see the world? Early in the last century, Estonian biologist Jakob Johann von Uexküll proposed the idea that organisms don't perceive the environment, or *Umgebung*, directly as it is, but a skewed version of it, constrained by their sense organs. He called this subjective world an *Umwelt*.[a] For example, a tick, which doesn't have eyes, sees the world by sensing butyric acid gradients given off by the sweat glands of mammals. When it senses high concentrations, it drops off its leaf tip, and if it is lucky enough to fall on a passing animal, which it can know by using its keen sense of temperature, it feels its way toward a hairless spot to attach and feed. This is the tick's entire world: butyric acid gradients, temperature, hair or no hair. In a broader sense, the worldview of any organism is constrained by not only its sense organs but also its evolved capacities and limitations for action and communication.

At one level, humans are no different: our worldview is limited by our five senses, by the things we can and can't do, and by the limits of our capacity for communication with others. We don't spend a lot of time thinking about navigating electrical gradients, flying, or reading the minds of animals, because we can't—at least unaided.

Yet there are some differences between the *Umwelten* of humans and other animals, which are important for harnessing individual and collective imagination. As individuals, we can be *aware* that our worldview is not complete or objective; we can deliberately *shape* it by learning, moving, and focusing our senses or our thoughts; and we can *extend* it by using technology to enhance our senses and capabilities. We can

OK—the first one to the top of the tree wins!

think of GPS, social media, and airplanes as "*Umwelt* stretchers," which extend our senses and capacities for socialization and action, and therefore our capacity for surprise and imagination.

At the collective level, we can understand and shape the *Umwelten* of others by using communication and by manipulating the organizational context, so that people in our business can share common experiences or be exposed to inspiring stimuli.

Each business has its own *Umwelt*. This might be narrow: one business might be obsessively focused on its price-earnings ratio or net promoter scores, like a tick, simply looking for the best place to extract value from its environment. Another business with a greater range of capacities and senses—things it measures and pays attention to—might be better at exploring the world, finding new niches, and reflecting on the limits of its own vision: wondering what is in the *Umgebung* that isn't in its *Umwelt*.

We *can* do things to expand and enrich and our individual and collective worldviews, but we don't necessarily do so suf-ficiently, consistently, deliberately, or skillfully. Choosing and learning to do so is a core idea of this book.

NOTE

a. J. von Uexküll, *A Foray into the Worlds of Animals and Humans with a Theory of Meaning* (Minneapolis, MN: University of Minnesota Press, 1934/2010).

Move Together

RELOCATE AND COLOCATE

Another way we can accelerate collective imagination around an idea is to move together in the world: to immerse our team in new geographical or social environments. For example, Google-owned company Jigsaw develops tools to address global security challenges to the internet such as hacking attacks and censorship. Jigsaw regularly sends groups of staff to develop their ideas by immersing themselves in relevant environments with key users of their products. Founder and CEO Jared Cohen uses the military term "human intelligence" to describe intelligence gained from the experience of individuals, as opposed to aggregated intelligence from data:

> [At this early stage] the bulk of the work is human intelligence and is deeply anthropological. This comes out of my background: I've done anthropological training and worked a lot in the intelligence community. We will come up with a set of hypotheses, sitting here. But then we will not pursue something or build something without forward deploying technical people into the field, to gut check our hypothesis . . . You will go to a country—if you work in anti-censorship, you will go to a country where censorship is really active—and you will talk to people, you will experience, you will play around.[23]

Probe Together

DISTRIBUTE AUTONOMY

Another way of sharing and amplifying evolving mental models is by probing the world together, to synchronize

Jared Cohen and the Jigsaw team getting out of the office and understanding how information flows work on the ground. *Source:* Courtesy of Jared Cohen.

Figure 6-8 Swisscom's prompt to give employees autonomy to develop imaginative ideas

Source: Presentation from David Hengartner, Head of Intrapreneurship at Swisscom/Cofounder and CEO at Getkickbox, 2020. Courtesy of Swisscom Kickbox.

exploration through experimentation. To enable this, businesses need to give employees some autonomy in terms of time and resources, so they can inspire others, bring together new teams, and try out new ideas.

Telecom company Swisscom has a system to support this: it gives people who have an imaginative suggestion a card to take to their manager, which starts a conversation about setting aside time over two months to develop the idea (see figure 6-8).

The online retail company Zappos is a pioneer in distributing autonomy. The company is composed of fifteen hundred employees in three hundred teams or "circles," each given power to determine what work they do and how to allocate their own budget based on the revenue they bring in. Anyone can create a new circle or pitch an idea to the head of any existing circle. Lead organizational designer John Bunch describes the system: "In the old world it only took one 'no' to shut something down, but in this world, it only take one 'yes' to get something started. So even if five hundred people say 'no, I'm not willing to fund that', but you pitched Tyler [who runs the brand team] and Tyler says 'that sounds like a crazy, amazing idea,' then, you know, it only takes one 'yes' to get something off the ground."[24]

Prototypes are another way to overcome the challenge of intersubjectivity: physically manifesting an idea in the world enables multiple imaginations to work collectively on it. As Apple's Ive noted: "When you make the very first physical manifestation of what the idea was, everything changes. It's the most profound shift. Because it's not exclusive anymore. It's not so open to interpretation. It's there, and it includes a lot of people."[25]

The goal for an imaginative company should be to distribute autonomy to build a portfolio of not-too-structured projects testing out imaginative ideas. For example:

- One employee researching a new approach to food in the café

- One bank branch testing out a floor redesign

- One team doing some ad hoc customer interviews around a new idea

- One partner running an experiment in augmented reality, and so on

They're from the R&D department—researching why companies should be led by R&D departments . . .

SUSPEND PRECISION

After an idea has spread to a small team and been tried out collectively, there comes a point when evaluative criteria need to be applied to determine if the idea warrants further support and amplification. This is tricky because of the intersubjectivity problem: How can you judge something when it is still a subjective model in someone's mind and likely not clearly defined and testable?

For well-developed projects, companies commonly apply financial metrics supported with detailed evidence and analysis. However, this is entirely the wrong approach for early-stage ideas. What we should do is reduce the requirement for precision around outcomes and vary our evaluation schemes according to the maturity of the idea. Eventually we will ask, "Will this help us be profitable?" On the journey to this point, though, we should ask:

1. *Does someone love it?* Roy Rosin, chief innovation officer at Penn Medicine, told us about this criterion. His first question about an early-stage idea is whether someone loves it and will push it to evolve. Does the idea have a champion? This rough measure helps guide what ideas should get an initial boost of support in terms of time or money.[26]

2. *What do other imaginative people think?* Mikael Dolsten, chief scientific officer and president, worldwide research, development and medical, of Pfizer Inc., identifies talented "concept builders" who have a track record of successfully rethinking mental models. He then asks them to give tentative opinions on early-stage ideas from their colleagues.[27]

3. *Does it show some interesting or promising result?* Determine whether efforts to act on the idea produce some interesting or promising effect. The result doesn't have to (yet) be superior to the current way of doing things, just a good starting point. For example, say that someone in the sales team at an office supplies company has the idea to sell basic first-aid kits, alongside stationery, to business clients. If a few clients express interest, this might be worth trying with a few more salespeople. Determining superiority—whether a full-scale addition to the company's offering would be profitable—can wait for a later stage.

4. *Is there a story you can tell about the path to success?* As an idea matures, we can ask those involved about whether they can describe a plausible path to success. Dolsten says, "They need to tell me why I should get convinced that this is on an upward trajectory. The bar at this point is, 'You need to be convinced that it's not hype, so it's not going to collapse.'"[28]

5. *Is it attracting followers?* If an idea manages to generate enthusiasm beyond the initial core of champions, this is a sign that it may warrant further resources and time spent on imagining—a criterion for early-stage funding in Recruit Holdings.

6. *Are people paying for it?* As experiments and prototypes develop, seeing people's willingness to pay on a small scale (before a full rollout) is another useful indicator, as we saw in our Turo example.

7. *Is it better than what exists?*
   This criterion perhaps comes to mind first when we assess counterfactual ideas. However, we should apply it only after an idea has satisfied all the previous criteria and has thus undergone an iterated process of reimagination and refinement and begun to achieve some of its technical potential.

Blocks to Collective Imagination

There are some common pathologies in corporations that prevent them collectively amplifying and evolving ideas.

Excessive Compliance

This is the pathology of following existing procedures and habits to the point of being closed to counterfactual ideas. It is what people often complain about as bureaucracy. Compliance often reduces the ability to listen imaginatively; the listener can't free themselves from the thought that "this clashes with existing procedures" enough to allow themselves to entertain a new idea. Novelty is regarded as threatening, and the new, counterfactual mental model remains stuck in one person's mind only. The solution: reinforce the thoughts that thinking is not doing and is thus low risk and

that what is now the status quo was originally novel and unfamiliar.

Cacophony

This is the pathology of sharing too many ideas without criteria for identifying the promising ones, meaning that good imaginative efforts get lost in the noise. Too much early-stage imagination, with no effort to select and amplify, is a much less common problem in large companies than a lack of imagination but can be equally detrimental to finding and focusing on new paths to growth. Antidotes include stage gates with prefinancial criteria, a back-burner status to put some ideas on hold, or predetermined time frames for projects.

Silos

Companies use specialization to scale, and people will always be grouped or group themselves into teams that develop their own identity. The problem comes when there is no countervailing force to balkanization, leading to fixed silos of activity—the business equivalent to lots of regional principalities ignoring or fighting with each other. There will always be groups and tensions between groups, but what supports imagination is a federal system, with a clear common interest and with mobility of thoughts and people. To create this, showcase and reward collaboration, recognize and support brokers, and allow new teams and working alliances to form spontaneously.

Depersonalization

Ideas get divorced from their champions. In a pandemic, we do a range of things to *stop* a virus spreading, the main one being to isolate carriers of a disease. With ideas, we want to achieve the opposite: for the carriers of imaginative mental models to infect as many people as possible. We undermine this possibility when the people behind imaginative ideas are socially distanced and not exposed to the mainstream of the company.

Games to Play

The Messy Foundations Game

Retiring executives of successful companies sometimes half-jokingly remark in their farewell speeches that they are not sure if the firm would hire them today. It's a self-deprecating joke; the implication is that the firm has gotten much better now. Yet the other possibility is that the firm is no longer hiring the sort of people who can help it grow.

This game is about remembering and appreciating the messiness at the foundational stage of the business and to recover that early mindset when the business was essentially

a counterfactual model, before everything became factual, familiar, and respectable.

Dig into the early history of your company and its founders and investigate how the foundational idea came about and how it was developed. Focus particularly on the mental aspect: What were the dominant beliefs of the day, and what was it like to imaginatively explore this new possibility at a time when not many other people thought that way? Go beyond the dates and data points to reconstruct the detailed human story of the events.

Once you have evoked what the previous commonsense mindset was versus the emerging imaginative challenge, improvise a conversation in which one person takes the part of skeptical realist of the time, and another person takes the part of the founder, trying to share her imaginative mental model of how things could be. Identify the kinds of blocks and objections that arise.

Then try the same thing but with a current big idea. Note which mental and social blocks are present today that prevent new ideas from flourishing.

The value of this game is to explore how your business started with a stop-and-start imaginative process, probably forgotten in the current professionalized operations, and to import some of that early-stage mindset into your leadership now. Start speculating about and exploring the potential next big transformation.

The Naming Game

Pick a still-developing imaginative idea of yours and name it in different ways, picking the most extreme version of:

- *Functionality:* equivalent to Griffiths Improved Vacuum Apparatus for Removing Dust from Carpets

- *Familiarity:* equivalent of the Apple Watch (even though it's not actually a watch)

- *Attracting attention:* the FCUK challenge

Swap ideas with a colleague and do the same for their idea. Compare results and pick your favorites. If it makes sense, announce your idea using the new name in an email to your team or more widely.

Good Questions to Ask

Some useful questions to ask in the amplification and diffusion stage of imagination are:

- How should we name the idea we're pursuing in a way that makes it comprehensible?

- What is the gripping story associated with the idea?

- Who is the hero of the new idea?

- What environments should the relevant team visit to further the idea?

- Do we celebrate brokers of ideas?

- Do we have appropriate criteria for assessing very early-stage ideas?

- Can employees easily share good ideas?

Organizational Diagnostic

We can take these actions and blocks and use them to determine if we are creating an environment that supports collective imagination. Each question is linked to a related action in this chapter.

		Never	Rarely or less than once a year	Sometimes or once a month to once a year	Usually or once a week to once a month	Always or more often than weekly
		(1)	(2)	(3)	(4)	(5)
	Related action					
Our firm gives names to (i.e., creates labels for) new, imaginative ideas.	Name things					
Employees use analogies, anecdotes, evocative descriptions, and other storytelling techniques, rather than just communicating information.	Train for storytelling					
People share ideas when they are still at an early, unformed, tentative stage.	Train for listening					
Employees make personal connections across different groups or business units in our company.	Support brokers					
We host forums for employees to present new projects and ideas.	Run a festival					
Our company makes decisions about new projects and funding in a decentralized way.	Distribute autonomy					
Nonsenior people in our firm bring together new teams to run experiments and pilot projects.	Distribute autonomy					
TOTAL						

After you have added up your total, you can score your current situation: 31–35, excellent; 21–30, good; 11–20, moderate; 0–10, poor. To benchmark your score against other organizations, please visit www.theimaginationmachine.org.

Chapter Seven

THE NEW ORDINARY

Before McDonald's, the world's first fast-food chain was White Castle. In Kansas in 1916, cook Walter Anderson set up a hamburger stand and invented a new way of serving hamburgers (making the patties thinner, putting onions on top). The trouble was, burgers were not popular due to health concerns—burgers at the time were mostly sold at lunch wagons and carnivals, with low-quality meat and poor hygiene.[1] Anderson had imagined and created a new hamburger, but to realize its potential, he needed to create the systems and processes to make take-out, fast-food hamburgers a new normal for millions of people.

Anderson met a business partner, Billy Ingram, a real estate and insurance agent, who envisaged a corporate empire with multiple interlocking businesses built around the new burger. In 1921, they set out to create this business, renaming their company White Castle System, Inc. (See figure 7-1.)

The White Castle System was a script—a set of instructions, articulated in manuals, booklets, posters, training programs, advertisements, and personal communications—to

Figure 7-1 Walt Anderson and Billy Ingram were the founders of the White Castle System®, the first fast-food chain

Source: © White Castle®. Reproduced by permission.

shape the thoughts and actions of many people in different roles, most of whom were not involved in the development of the original idea, many of whom Anderson and Ingram would never even meet. As the Kansas Historical Society notes: "White Castle proved successful because the company developed standards of operation. Anderson created paper hats, paper wrapped hamburgers, a manual for food preparation, and guidelines for employee cleanliness and appearance."[2] (See figure 7-2.)

The system included a number of elements: a simple menu, cheap pricing strategy, intense marketing, as well as a standardized cooking process, uniform codes, and regularly cleaned, enamel buildings.[3] No one had built a fast-food chain before, so the infrastructure didn't exist. Anderson and

Figure 7-2 A White Castle® interior, 1947
Source: © White Castle®. Reproduced by permission.

Figure 7-3 White Castle®, 2020

Source: Universal Images Group North America LLC/Alamy Stock Photo.

Ingram created what we would today call a business ecosystem; they built meat supply plants, bakeries, and two supporting businesses: Paperlynen, to make paper products for the restaurants, and Porcelain Steel Buildings, to make their unique prefabricated porcelain walls. By 1931, White Castle had 131 outlets; in 1961, it became the first restaurant to sell one billion burgers; today it continues, a hundred years after founding.[4] (See figure 7-3.) Although the business was eventually overtaken in size by others, it shaped an entire industry.

• • •

White Castle's growth illustrates that if you want to harness collective imagination, you need to turn your imaginative

mental model into a new normal, which for an existing company involves a wholesale transformation. This chapter will explore the idea of an evolvable script as the means for doing this, best practices for creating such scripts, blocks to doing so, productive games to play, questions to ask, and an organizational diagnostic.

The Challenge of Reshaping Reality

How can you shape a new reality? When we think about corporations, we tend to focus on the material aspects—the products, warehouses, shop fronts, labs, impressive headquarters, and so on. But as we touched on in chapter 4, businesses are predicated on mental models. For example, LEGO, at one point, was not a thing, and now it is, not only because some factories have manufactured colored bricks. If you gave some LEGO bricks to a cave man in 30,000 BC, he wouldn't know what to do with them. LEGO products shaped the world because the LEGO Group created a script that shaped the minds of the people making up the company and its customers. The *mental* side of the product has been articulated and spread; there is a widely understood mental model of what these colored objects are and how to use them, all organized under a now-familiar name, LEGO, which at one point in history meant nothing.

What's extraordinary about corporations is that they come from the mind but have a massive power to reshape reality. A rough estimate of the total weight of all iPhones ever made is 374 million kilograms (2.2 billion phones at an average of 170 grams each): raw materials that have been excavated, transformed, and sent around the world in people's pockets. Even the sternest critics of corporations, Karl Marx and Friedrich Engels, were not able to resist a sense of awe:

> The bourgeoisie, during its rule of scarce one hundred years, has created more massive and more colossal productive forces than have all preceding generations together. Subjection of Nature's forces to man, machinery, application of chemistry to industry and agriculture, steam-navigation, railways, electric tele-graphs, clearing of whole continents for cultivation, canalization of rivers, whole populations conjured out of the ground—what earlier century had even a pre-sentiment that such productive forces slumbered in the lap of social labor?[5]

It is easy to let the power of such corporations—Apple, Samsung, GE, Exxon Mobil, Nike, or others—lead us to believe that their identity and their power derive from mate-rial things. Yet a company does not even have the material solidity of a simple object, like a shoe. If you take a shoe off, you can put it in the corner, and it will stay that way until it slowly degrades and, eventually, returns to dust. A company's essence is not tied to matter: it is a set of interrelated mental models in people's brains, shaped by a corporate script. A company would evaporate within days if people no longer wanted or needed to play their roles within it.

At the heart of the corporation is a mental operating system that holds everything together: a script that can be articulated in rules and processes and strategy, but that is run on people's brains. Writing and enacting such a script is how we reshape reality. When a script is running, it creates an institution, a corporation that orchestrates large amounts of resources and makes new mental models and actions fa-miliar, so eventually they become the fabric of a new reality. Eventually, the White Castle System created a new ordinary in which millions of people buy burgers—from ubiquitous outlets supported by large supply chains—assuming without question that the food will be safe and tasty.

How can we learn to do this well? How can we turn our imagined mental model into the basis of a new everyday reality?

Our imaginative project succeeded. I'm pleased to report everyone finds it dull and ordinary now.

How to Write Evolvable Scripts

We might see policies and procedures as the end, even the antithesis, of imagination. But institutionalizing an idea is in fact a different type of imaginative challenge because we have to use counterfactual thinking to picture the new reality and the corporate machine that will bring it about. The White Castle System was an extraordinary achievement of grounded counterfactual thinking: a script for a never-before-seen kind of business, which was clear enough to guide others and actually worked in practice.

By corporate script, we mean any kind of guidance that drives thought and action. For example, let's say you are running a movie theater company, and you reimagine the mental model for how a theater should run. Following this, you need to write the script for the new theaters and supplemental services—guidance and instruction you will communicate to the franchisees, customers, and vendors who will create and live within the new normal.

There are three steps to creating and running an effective corporate script: understand, articulate, and evolve.

Understand

First, we need to grasp the essential value of the imaginative idea we have created—the key ingredients and causal relationships, and what is merely incidental. This is the essential value we want to capture and codify in the script.

REFLECT AFTER SUCCESS

Usually when something *doesn't* work, we spend time figuring out what happened. But avoiding failure is not success. And success does not automatically mean repeated success. In fact, succeeding is usually more complex and mysterious than failing, as it involves a system of successful interactions, whereas failure usually involves one or a few things going wrong.

Losers in a competition often take a break to enter a period of soul searching. Ideally, *success* should also trigger reflection and soul searching, as this is the best time to reverse-engineer why something worked so it can be replicated.

At the BCG Henderson Institute, we ring a bell after any major success. The bell signals the need not only to celebrate but also to pause and reflect, to codify what went right (see figure 7-4). The team then meets to explore everything that led to the moment of success and capture this in our recipe book (simple, evolvable scripts) for important routines, such as how we research and develop a new idea. A similar policy could be adopted in any business as a starting point for codifying new scripts.

IDENTIFY THE ESSENCE

Once we have made time to reflect after success, a key action is to identify the essence of why something worked. For example, in the late 1990s, Adidas explored the idea of personalizing footwear. The team harnessed imagination effectively: they rethought the experience of buying a shoe, tried this out, rethought, and did further pilots. Then, they drilled down to identify the essence of what was successful in these

Not usually considered a time for soul-searching. *Source:* PA Images/Alamy Stock Photo.

An imaginative, thoughtful team, after a success—thinking hard about what went right. *Source:* Claudio Villa/Getty Images Sport via Getty Images.

tests. They discovered that consumers were more concerned about customized fit than customized design, something they hadn't expected. This was the starting point for writing a new organizational script, which Adidas eventually enacted to transform thousands of stores.[6]

Another example of extracting essential principles of success comes from educator Maria Montessori. Early in the twentieth century, she turned her ideas about education from one-off successes into a script that others could follow. As director of a school in Rome, she noticed one child who was having difficulty learning how to sew. She tried a few things out and discovered that the girl, while she struggled with sewing, enjoyed weaving pieces of paper together.[7] Montessori focused on the task the student enjoyed. Later, the

girl picked up sewing. This was an imaginative success for Montessori. But it became more than a one-off success because she mined such encounters for essential principles (see figure 7-5).

From this small success, she drew a key insight: "We should really find the way to teach the child *how*, before making her execute a task . . . by means of repeated exercises not in the work itself but in that which *prepares* for it."[8] This became the principle of a "prepared environment" in the overall script: the Montessori Method. This method made the difference between one school in Rome shaped by reimagination and a scalable script, now followed by around twenty thousand schools around the world—the most widespread method in education.[9]

Figure 7-4 The bell to ring to discuss what led to success

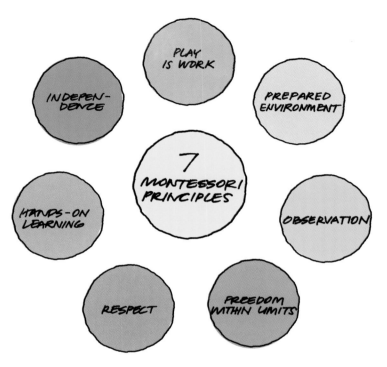

Figure 7-5 The seven Montessori principles

To take another example, when Ingram examined Anderson's successful hamburger stand, he noticed that one essential element was the cleanliness. They enshrined this in the White Castle System, communicated to employees on posters in every outlet (see figure 7-6).

This element of the script also shaped their communications with customers, in castle-shaped booklets, emphasizing that the food is "protected constantly by modern electrical refrigeration, served in spotlessly clean castles" (see figure 7-7).

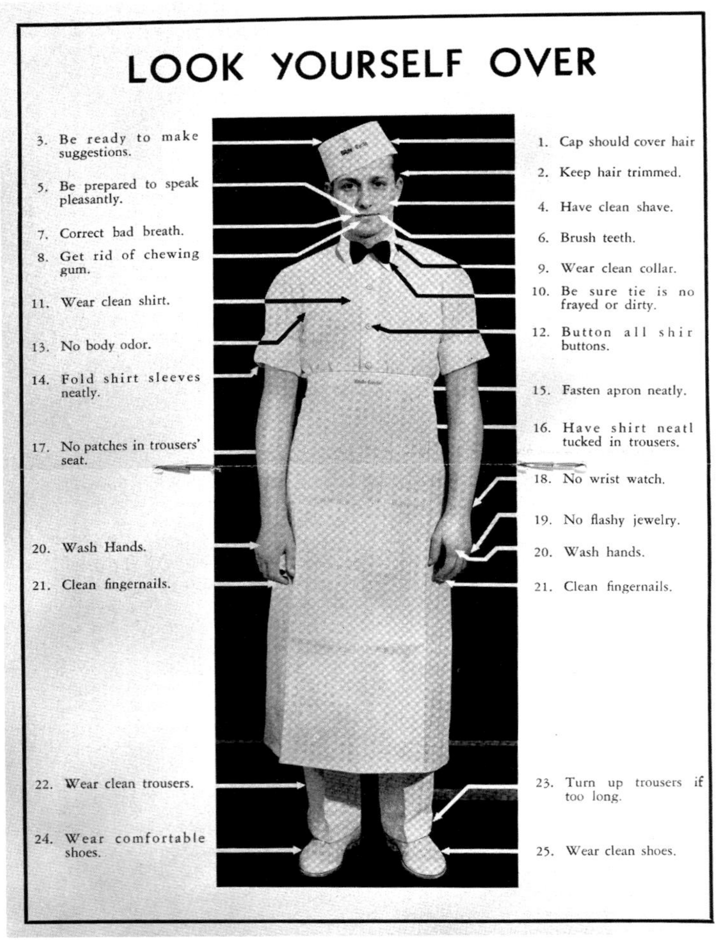

LOOK YOURSELF OVER

3. Be ready to make suggestions.

5. Be prepared to speak pleasantly.

7. Correct bad breath.

8. Get rid of chewing gum.

11. Wear clean shirt.

13. No body odor.

14. Fold shirt sleeves neatly.

17. No patches in trousers' seat.

20. Wash Hands.

21. Clean fingernails.

22. Wear clean trousers.

24. Wear comfortable shoes.

1. Cap should cover hair

2. Keep hair trimmed.

4. Have clean shave.

6. Brush teeth.

9. Wear clean collar.

10. Be sure tie is no frayed or dirty.

12. Button all shir buttons.

15. Fasten apron neatly.

16. Have shirt neatl tucked in trousers.

18. No wrist watch.

19. No flashy jewelry.

20. Wash hands.

21. Clean fingernails.

23. Turn up trousers if too long.

25. Wear clean shoes.

Figure 7-6 Essential to the White Castle® corporate recipe: hygiene and a clean appearance

White Castle® appearance chart, 1956. *Source:* © White Castle®. Reproduced by permission.

To others in the mass-market food industry of that day, focusing on cleanliness would *not* have seemed obvious or essential. Customers didn't expect it; most cooks and owners probably saw their role as just serving the food, perhaps chatting with patrons. The clarity, confidence, and independence of mind to highlight and focus on this laid the groundwork for a successful corporate script that would transform the entire industry.

To distinguish the essential from the incidental, we should focus on elements that are:

- Critical to success

- Nonobvious

- Difficult; that is, which require an explicit script

- Differentiated from similar things in the world

- Generative; that is, if you get this one thing right, many other good things will likely follow

Articulate

Once we have understood what is essential to the success of a newly imagined idea, we need to articulate these elements in a corporate script: the more- or less-specific guidance required so that people who have no knowledge of or experience with the mental model, and may not be immediately inspired by it, are able to play their part in realizing it. (See the sidebar "Elements of Corporate Scripts.")

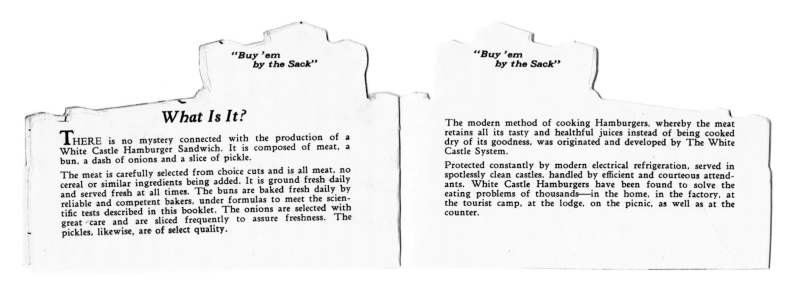

Figure 7-7 Shaping the mental models of customers

White Castle® brochure, 1932. *Source:* © White Castle®. Reproduced by permission.

CLARIFY THE PURPOSE

In order to frame the specifics of who does what, you must first specify your purpose. A purpose is a kind of goal—a description of what you hope to bring about. It is the goal for the overall effort. To describe the purpose, identify the intersection of your:

- *Aspirations:* the exciting possibility you have envisaged with your mental model

- *Capabilities:* what is possible given the resources you might access now and in the future

- *Context:* the jobs to be done within the broader system of which you are a part

A key function of a purpose is to stop people blindly pursuing some tactical part of the script while losing sight of the intention of the whole. In his 2016 letter to shareholders, Amazon CEO Jeff Bezos wrote that leaders must "resist proxies," meaning "the process is not the thing."[10] A proxy is an intermediate goal, like "reduce maintenance costs" in an industrial equipment company, on which you can end up focusing a lot effort, but which is not the overall goal. The danger with proxies is that you end up skewing the collective

Elements of Corporate Scripts

What are the different elements that you can put into a corporate or institution-building script? The elements are different kinds of guidance to shape people's mental models and actions (communicated via manuals, presentations, training sessions, implicit instructions built into design, marketing materials, personal discussions, and so on) that result in the creation of a new reality.

We can picture the possible elements for a script as parts of a house. At the top is a *purpose*. This overall goal connects a business to the social system it is embedded in by delineating some useful contribution to individual or collective flourishing, orienting the entire business and serving as an aspiration for future growth. For example, a reimagined bank could have as a purpose to help us be happier and wiser about money across all the ways money impacts our lives.

Under the purpose is *strategy*, which is everything it takes to win competitively, in pursuit of the purpose, and *goals and metrics*, which specify targets within the strategy and enable us to assess progress.

Under this are a range of possible elements we can add into scripts that specify how this purpose will be achieved in detail:

- **Principles:** Key pieces of guidance that can be applied in many situations. For example, "customer-facing staff in the hotel should use their discretion when they can see a way to solve a guest's problem."

- **Rules:** Descriptions of specific behaviors to enact or avoid. For example, "clean the restaurant every two hours."

- **Protocols:** Codes of conduct comprising principles and rules. The term "protocol" comes from diplomacy; for example: "the following twenty-five rules and six principles should be followed in order to orchestrate a state dinner." In business, we might have protocols for running an investor call, engaging a new customer, conducting a recruiting interview, and so on.

- **Processes:** Series of actions intended to produce particular results or kinds of results. For example: the sequence of steps for cooking a beef patty, assembling a car, analyzing customer metrics, or testing a new drug.

- **Role descriptions:** Priorities and responsibilities of personal roles. For example, "this reimagined real estate company depends on estate agents with the skills to handle the following responsibilities: emotional engagement with the client, design advice, and help with financial planning."

Within each of these ways of giving guidance lie *critical details* vital to success. For example, the exact length of time to cook a burger, the ideal temperature of a store during shopping hours, the minimum inventory levels for a factory, the need for all toys to be intercompatible, or the threshold for the efficacy of a drug.

Finally, one important aspect of the script is its *evolvability*. This is the capacity for the script to adapt in response to change and surprise. We will explore the theme of evolvability later in the chapter.

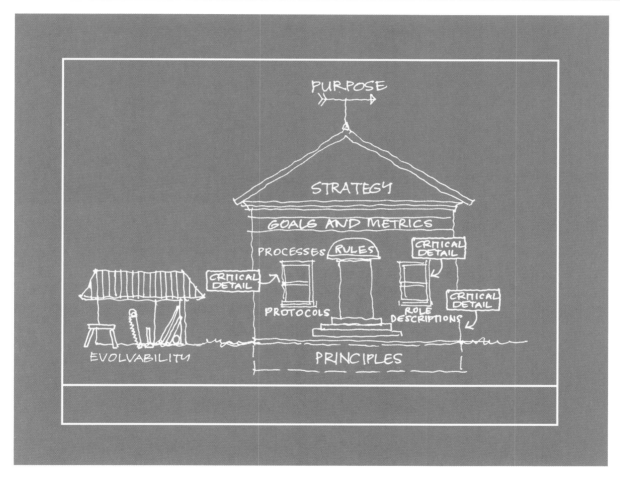

Possible elements of corporate scripts

But if we let the customers in, sir, we'll never keep the temperature in the shop at the required level!

effort, if from your perspective, for example, it becomes irrelevant whether customers hire your equipment or whether you have any inventory.*

FOCUS SCRIPT ON ACTION

When articulating elements of the script that will guide people to shape the new reality, it is tempting to focus on description, explanation, or justification. But whether you are communicating it through a corporate manual, onboarding training, or personal communication, every piece of the script should be oriented around prompting and guiding action.

To see what makes a good script, imagine three different sports coaches, each trying to train beginner athletes to jump over a vaulting horse.

How do you write a script for doing this? *Source:* Nationaal Archief (Dutch National Archives), via Creative Commons. Photograph by Sterling/Anefo.

1. The first coach tells students to "optimize your velocity and angle of attack relative to the height of the object." (He continues with a lecture about mass and momentum.)

2. The second coach says simply, "Empty your mind."

3. The third coach tells students to "lean against the edge of your chair and push the weight of your body up and down with your arms and remember this sensation as you run up to the vaulting horse."

Which coach is likely to be the most effective? The first is technically correct, but his instructions were too complicated to guide action in real time. This often happens in corporate scriptwriting. In one BCG project, we worked on an operational assessment of a pharmaceutical company. The com-

---

*Examples from machine intelligence illustrate this at an extreme level because AI is good at goals that are tied to a particular task but not good at interpreting overall statements of purpose. In the book *Superintelligence,* philosopher Nick Bostrom gives an imaginary example of a hyperintelligent computer that is given the goal "make paper clips" and ends up using every possible resource toward that end, eventually consuming the Earth, then turning large portions of the universe into paper clips.

"Consider mass velocity . . ."   "Empty your mind."   "Push up off a chair."

Right—we have a deep appreciation of the vision—but does anyone know how to turn the fryer on?

pany had hundreds of pages of procedures and protocols for managing safety—in theory, the script for how the machine of the company should run in enormous detail. But no one understood it because it was too much for anyone to even read.

The second coach's recipe is indeed simple—"empty your mind"—but useless for instructing people who are not already trained athletes. The business equivalent might be a vice president asking their CEO, "How should I scale up this program to a thousand stores across Latin America?" and getting the answer, "Just go for it. Be bold. Believe in yourself."

The third coach's recipe is what we should be aiming for. She figured out the essential actions that mattered most—the muscle movements really are the key to vaulting—and described it in a way that anyone could follow.

A great example of memorable, action-oriented code is Apple's rules for store employees: **A**pproach, **P**robe, **P**resent, **L**isten, **E**nd:

- Approach customers with a personalized warm welcome.

- Probe politely to understand all the customer's needs.

- Present a solution for the customer to take home today.

- Listen for and resolve any issues or concerns.

- End with a fond farewell and an invitation to return.

This beautifully simple code is written to be comprehended and used. Within Apple stores, it is called the "credo," and employees meet daily to discuss one of the five steps and share examples with the team.[11]

Complex sets of rules don't transmit information effectively, and people do not understand or use them. When scriptwriting, we should think like a sports coach at half-time:

we have a few minutes of others' attention to use words and diagrams to guide observation, thought, and behavior.

DEPLOY REALISTS

In articulating a script, one valuable move is to involve people who can think pragmatically about how something might work and what could go wrong. Investor Bill Janeway emphasizes the value of *grounded* imagination: "I think of imagination as constructive and productive when it is grounded in a multidimensional appreciation of where we are and therefore from where we're beginning."[12]

People who think of themselves as imaginative and those who think of themselves as realists don't usually work well together. But one way to think about realists is that they are people with a particular bent to their imagination: because of their awareness of the complexity of reality, their counterfactual thinking focuses on the challenges of implementation. Imagination is a calibrated departure from the current mental model of reality: too realistic and there is no innovation; too unrealistic and it becomes an impractical fantasy. The ideal calibration varies according to the maturity of the mental model. Deploying realists too early can suppress idea development. Deploying them at the point of codifying a corporate script can be productive. In the Adidas example of personalized footwear, such a person's mind might jump to:

- The difficulty of working with retail partners around the world, given differing expectations about who will pay for the new equipment

- The challenge of fitting customization into Adidas's existing departments; thus the need to rethink Adidas's structure as part of codifying this program

- The difficulty of doing customized manufacturing in Adidas's existing factories

Involving minds focused on the trickiness of current reality will help articulate a script for thought and action that will effectively reshape reality.

Evolve

An overall consideration in writing a corporate script is to design it so that it can evolve, to change in response to changing demands or opportunities.

ALLOW DISCRETION

One way to enhance evolvability is to allow for individual discretion. Institutional scripts always have the potential to turn people into (unintelligent) robots: when they interpret the code as "follow these instructions and do not think." Instead, a corporate code should make room for and draw on the imaginations of the people enacting it.

As we noted in the previous chapter, online retail company Zappos does this effectively. The script that drives the company is called "Holocracy" and involves largely autonomous teams that function like startups.[13] Employees can join or leave teams at will, and teams and individuals can write

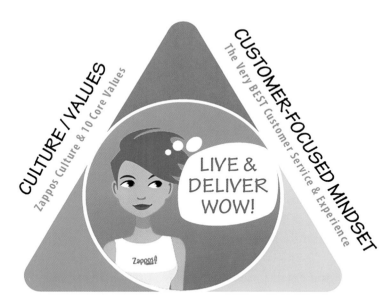

CUSTOMER-GENERATED BUDGETING

Balance Your Circle's P&L

Figure 7-8 Zappos's Triangle of Accountability

Source: Courtesy of Zappos.

new corporate script. As founder Tony Hsieh said to us, "If an employee wants to start up a circle to set up a cupcake bakery, that would be great. The only demand is that this bakery abides by our purpose to deliver the very best customer service, customer experience, and company culture."[14]

This level of discretion is balanced by an additional key piece of corporate script: the Triangle of Accountability, which codifies criteria by which each team must guide itself. (See figure 7-8.)

Another example of creating room for discretion is the Four Seasons hotel chain. When building the global corporate machine in the 1980s, founder Isadore Sharp faced a challenge of corporate scriptwriting: how to identify the essence of his early hotels and build on it to create a global chain based around core, shared mental models. Sharp believed that frontline employees were key to the hotel experience. He wanted to invest enough in training and supporting frontline staff to justify trusting them to improvise or bend rules to solve customer problems. Sharp wrote a credo articulating this: "It took most of the first half of the 1980s to clear out

Room 15 wants to bathe in asses' milk . . .

all the obstacles that stood in the way of improving service: to part ways with every executive who believed my 'kooky' credo should be confined to the PR department, to part ways with every executive whose actions contradicted policy."[15]

Sharp's policy, a key piece of the corporate script, now underpins the operations of over a hundred hotels worldwide. One employee noted how the principles shaped the reality: "I have countless stories about how this philosophy played out. A bartender once sent me to a corner bar to pick up a six-pack of Rolling Rock even though it wasn't on our beer menu. I knew a doorman who jumped in a cab to return a lost teddy bear to a kid at the airport. People spoke of the

Typically, you should love one another.

That's open to interpretation . . .

Room Service waiter who borrowed blueberries from another hotel at 3 a.m. because we ran out."[16]

You should include enough room for discretion in your institutional recipe so the imaginations of the people involved aren't underutilized.

EVOLVE EXISTING SCRIPTS

Another challenge is not just to evolve the script you are newly writing but other preexisting scripts to which it relates. When you are transforming a company or designing a new department around a new product, a new script often runs up against established ones.

Media entrepreneur John Battelle has an example of this challenge from the perspective of an outsider. Battelle had thought of a new business model, and he wanted to partner with a large company. He approached the company, and even though it saw the merit in his idea, the company was unable to transform its existing protocols to do anything about it:

> We approached the company with our business idea: we wanted to get access to some of their discarded product. We said: "We want to give you a piece of our equity for the rights to this stuff you are discarding. You don't have to do anything for it. In fact, our venture will probably help increase your customer base. It is free for you. How could you say no to this?"
>
> So of course, they took the meetings, they got excited. But then they threw it over to their legal department, and the CFO's office, because legal has to approve any deals. That's where it hit the rocks. They did not know how to do it, within their protocols. They even admitted this to us in the room. They said: "This is a great idea. But we don't know how to do a deal where we own a minority stake in a company. Give us something we're used to doing."[17]

The company was unable to make room within its established script—its existing operating system—for an imaginative, valuable new effort.

White Castle® challenging its own script. *Source:* Courtesy of Miso Robotics.

A new corporate script: White Castle® in collaboration with Miso Robotics. *Source:* Courtesy of Miso Robotics.

In another example, White Castle has recently begun to experiment with using AI-driven robots in its kitchens, a move that has the potential to disrupt its existing corporate script.

This effort is currently at the formative stages of imagination: collective imagination and experimentation. But it could become the basis for envisaging a wholly new script for White Castle, part of which (written in actual computer code) is run on robot arms in the kitchens, with the human scripts (written into training programs and key principles) guiding employees around customer engagement. Anderson and Ingram's White Castle System from 1921 would have to evolve, merging with new, AI-augmented scripts, leading, once everything becomes familiar and habitual, to a "new ordinary."

An established script is the operating system, the software, on which the company runs. This software must be updatable. As well as imagining new script, we should be ready to evolve the old.

ERASE SCRIPTS

One ongoing and often neglected task in any corporate system is to trim rules and protocols to contain complexity within a tractable range.[18] For example, Netflix has a rule to eliminate unnecessary rules: "As we grow, minimize rules."[19] CEO Reed Hastings and chief talent officer Patty McCord codified their approach in a slide deck on best practices for Human Resources, which Facebook COO Sheryl Sandberg has called "one of the most important documents ever to come out of Silicon Valley."[20] A key principle it emphasizes is to "eliminate distracting complexity (barnacles)" and "value simplicity." The document discusses "rule creep": "'Bad' processes tend to creep in—preventing errors just sounds so good. We try to get rid of rules where we can, to reinforce the point."[21]

Trader Joe's also has an effective script erasure process: keeping its total number of products stable by removing the old as it introduces the new. In this way, there are never so many products that workers don't know enough about each one to be able to discuss it with customers.

Erasing script comes from seeing the whole. Even if a particular rule might be justified by some local need, we should never forget to weigh this against the need for the company script as a whole to function—to remain understandable and evolvable.

We were able to reduce maintenance costs to zero by getting rid of the factory altogether!

Blocks to Evolvable Scripts

There are a number of commonly encountered obstacles to imagining and enacting evolvable corporate scripts, especially when the starting point is within an existing large business.

Being Excessively Procedural

This is the habit of thinking only according to tightly defined procedures, preventing evolvability. This pathology can develop from the fear of punishment for doing something wrong, or an excessive attachment to clarity and an aversion to ambiguity. The antidotes are to reinforce the purpose as the true goal, rather than the procedures, and to support people in going off-script when they think it makes sense, despite missteps that may occur.

Being Overly Producer Focused

This is the tendency to forget that the point is to create value for the customer and so forgetting to design based on the customer's experience. It gives rise to rules and procedures that make sense from a partial, internal perspective (someone in procurement or the finance team) but that neglect the customer, and so stop the script from being effective for customers, whose lives it is designed to make better. The solution: regularly talk to customers, go through the process

Philosophies of Instruction

A script is a means of instructing or guiding people. All scripts should be evolvable, to some degree, and all scripts should specify something to be done. Evolvability is the degree to which the script itself changes, is erased, or is added to over time. Specificity is the degree to which the script tightly defines actions, versus leaving room for interpretation and imagination. The two are linked: writing a script that leaves lots of room for discretion helps prompt the imagination that may help the script evolve more over time. But there are a number of possible approaches along these dimensions.

What factors drive the choice of approach? Evolvability versus rigidity depends on how likely the value proposition is to change over time. In business environments that are unpredictable or newly emerging, it makes sense to make corporate scripts that are designed to change. The scripts' specificity versus generality depend on the degree to which people's imagination is required to realize the value proposition and on how critical the precise details are to success. To ensure consistency of customer experience across a franchise business or in relation to safety rules, it makes sense to be very specific. When people need to improvise or customize to create value because customer needs are varied or subtle, it makes sense for scripts to be more general.

Let's look at some examples. You might create a script that specifies in detail the required ways of thinking and behaving, not designed to evolve much over time, such as the original White Castle System. When Four Seasons founder Isadore Sharp spent a day sitting in on a McDonald's training ses-

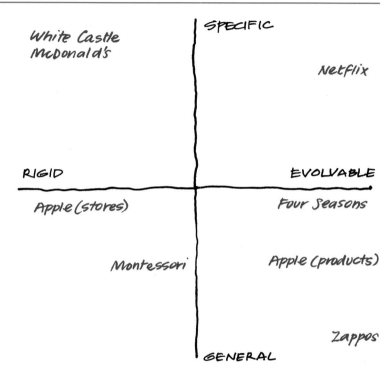

Trade-offs in corporate scriptwriting

sion in the 1960s (he admired McDonald's and was trying to learn lessons from its script), he noted that the materials were fifteen to twenty years old. "It struck me then that when you have something people can identify with, you don't have to keep reinventing it; once it's rooted, it sticks."[a] McDonald's bets on the fact that people will want cheeseburgers for a long time. And it requires accuracy, not imagination, to make one. The best script elements to employ in this case are rules, protocols, and detailed role descriptions.

Alternately, you might write an institution-building script with more general guidance, but still relatively rigid. Examples include Montessori's method: the core principles of how to educate a human being are intended to remain the bedrock, but these can be interpreted imaginatively by teachers in different circumstances. Apple's script for its retail stores is another example. The stores have a credo of general but largely unchanging principles. Good in-person retail service is a pretty permanent value proposition, but which requires latitude for on-the-ground interpretation by employees. Principles are the go-to element in this kind of script, as well as key metrics, all linked to an overall purpose. A good way of communicating these is via observation and mentorship, to learn how the principles can play out in different circumstances.

Another approach to scriptwriting is to create a general *and* evolvable script. Zappos, for example, specifies very little, other than to be nice to customers, follow the company culture, and balance your P&L. Everything else changes, and even this high-level script is intended to evolve as the company and the meaning of an excellent customer experience evolves. This allows Zappos to define and pursue new value propositions, drawing on the imagination of staff members as they go. The script behind some of Apple's products (as opposed to its stores) also embodies this logic. The ecosystem of iPhone, App Store, developer, and customer is built from processes and protocols that are designed to evolve as new needs and apps emerge. The best way to communicate a script like this is by clearly setting the purpose and being specific about some core aspects of how the platform works (listing, pricing, profit sharing, branding, and the like) but letting market principles play out for the assortment of apps.

Finally, a script can also combine specificity and evolvability. One example is Netflix, which operates in a fast-changing industry, but which still needs to define specific guidance across its business units to deliver on its (evolving) value proposition. Its solution has been to enshrine a specific rule for removing rules. To create this kind of script, you can draw on all the elements, from purpose to processes to specific rules. Evolvability depends on constantly revisiting the script.

NOTE

a. Isadore Sharp, *Four Seasons* (New York: Penguin Publishing Group, 2009), 92. For the date of this anecdote, see: Sheridan Prasso, "Four Season's Recession-Proof Philosophy," *CNN Money*, May 7, 2009, https://money.cnn.com/2009/05/06/news/newsmakers/prasso_sharp.fortune/index.htm.

from their perspective, and rewrite the corporate script as required.

Desire for Control

This is the temptation to imagine that we can specify everything in advance. It often derives from a worry about what might ensue if there aren't enough rules, without actually testing out this possibility. The anxiety can become the driver of rulemaking rather than the goal of creating something valuable. One countermeasure is to track the adoption and usefulness of the rules in practice and to trim unnecessary complexity. One can also experiment to see if more easily understood and more flexible principle-based guidance give superior outcomes to explicit and complex rules.

Trying to Be Completely "MECE"

This pathology is the belief that every list, document, and set of principles must be mutually exclusive and collectively exhaustive (MECE), leading to an uncontrolled blooming of specifications, descriptions, and rules for contingencies. The antidote is to remember that, while the principle MECE has its applications, the point of a script is not to be exhaustive; it is to be communicable and usable, even enjoyable to read or communicate, to prompt the few actions that matter most, rather than covering every eventuality.

Games to Play

The No-Friction Game

Imagine a business like yours but one where customers experience no friction: perfect choice, perfect information, no search costs, perfect understanding of your offering, perfect availability, no mistakes, no quality issues or rework, and no delays. Then observe where your actual business departs from this ideal scenario. Consider the cost of the current frictions. Then ask yourself: What sources of friction are largest and most tractable to eliminate or substantially reduce?

If you have a script for how you will scale up and deliver a new imaginative idea, consider it in this context: How will this new corporate script help ad-dress the existing sources of friction? Or if you don't, think about what sort of script could bring about such a reduction in friction.

Of course, no business is friction-free. But disruptors, to have a viable and compelling proposition, will necessarily address a source of friction that incumbents take for granted. It can be hard to identify such frictions since the current business model may have decades of precedent and seem reasonable or unavoidable. There may be no customers complaining about or competitors yet addressing these frictions. You might imagine a friction-free insurance company, for example. Comparing your current company to this ideal, you could ask: Is it inevitable that there are many risks that are hard to insure, that insurance contracts are hard to understand, that it's hard for individuals to comprehend their total risk profile, that it's painful to adjust one's insurance portfolio, that intermediaries take substantial margins for providing navigation and advice, and that claims are resolved only after a substantial delay? As you write a transformational script for your company, you can be guided by reducing such frustrations. Addressing frictions generally involves not only adding novelty but eliminating complexity in the existing scripts that guide your business.

The Codification Game

The task of translating an imagined new thing into a script that will guide others to realize that new thing is a difficult one. To practice this on a small scale with colleagues, make some object, like a castle, out of LEGO bricks. When you have finished, don't show this object to the others. Instead, in words, describe the object and how others should recreate

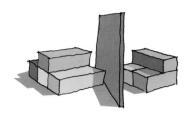

it (the script). Their task is then to build that object out of LEGO bricks, based only on the script.

To take the game to another level, different teams can compete with different scriptwriting philosophies. One team could specify every action with detailed rules. Another could describe the core principles only. And another could focus on communicating just the overall purpose or outcome. You can also change the objective from the most accurate reproduction to the fastest adequate model to the most interesting model to the one that is the most fun to make, and so on.

You can extract lessons about how different scriptwriting approaches and behavioral biases can help or hinder the translation of an idea into reality. You can then apply these lessons to transforming part or all of your existing corporate script in light of a promising, imaginative idea.

Good Questions to Ask

Some good questions to ask in writing the script that will scale your imaginative efforts are:

- What's the minimum someone would need to know to execute and deliver the new idea successfully?

- What is the purpose of this set of procedures?

- Where do people need to use discretion within this script?

- What customer experience are the procedures designed to deliver?

- In addition to writing, how will we deliver the script and reinforce it to those using it?

- Is the trade-off between completeness and comprehensibility optimal?

Organizational Diagnostic

You can apply this diagnostic to your organization to get a sense of how effectively you create and manage corporate scripts. Each question is linked to a related action in this chapter that you can turn to if you need to work on that area.

	Related action	Never	Rarely or less than once a year	Sometimes or once a month to once a year	Usually or once a week to once a month	Always or more often than weekly
		(1)	(2)	(3)	(4)	(5)
Employees take time after successes to reflect on why that outcome happened.	Reflect after success					
The firm translates one-off successes into general principles or rules to follow.	Identify the essence					
Our company's purpose statement is useful and provokes imagination.	Clarify the purpose					
A typical employee knows and uses our corporate principles and institutional knowledge.	Focus script on action					
In general, individual employees in our firm balance visionary and realist tendencies.	Deploy realists					
Our corporate codes allow for individual discretion.	Allow discretion					
Our firm has an explicit process that it regularly uses for removing unnecessary rules.	Erase script					
TOTAL						

After you have added up your total, score your current situation: 31–35, excellent; 21–30, good; 11–20, moderate; 0–10, poor. To benchmark your score against other organizations, please visit www.theimaginationmachine.org.

Chapter Eight

THE ENCORE

Amazon is a much-talked-about company, but it does powerfully illustrate a crucial point: the possibility of sustaining successive and successful acts of imagination over time, continuously finding new paths to growth even as a company grows very large. Amazon has continually imagined and created new businesses, starting with a mental model of "Earth's biggest bookstore" in 1995; reimagining itself as an "everything store"; opening up its platform to third-party sellers in 2000; starting cloud computing in 2006; developing a physical product, Kindle, in 2007; creating a film and TV studio in 2010; and launching an AI-driven store with no checkouts, Amazon Go, in 2018. It has incorporated widely different business models across eighty-eight acquisitions, ranging from game-streaming platform Twitch to home security company Ring to supermarket Whole Foods, and has even explored radical company operating model philosophies via the acquisition of online retailer Zappos.[1]

Amazon has been sustainably successful because it has combined two mentalities: efficiency and imagination. CEO Jeff Bezos contrasts this with companies that invent something on Day 1 and then live off this for Day 2 and beyond, leading to eventual stasis and decline. Bezos said, "This kind of decline would happen in extreme slow motion. An established company might harvest Day 2 for decades, but the final result would still come."[2] To avoid this fate, your business must combine harvesting well-cultivated areas with exploring counterfactual landscapes. Bezos describes the combination:

> Sometimes (often actually) in business, you *do* know where you're going, and when you do, you can be efficient. In contrast, wandering in business is not efficient . . . but it's also not random. It's *guided*—by hunch, gut, intuition, curiosity, and powered by a deep conviction that the prize for customers is big enough that it's worth being a little messy and tangential to find our way there. Wandering is an essential counterbalance to efficiency. You need to employ both. The

outsized discoveries—the "nonlinear" ones—are highly likely to require wandering.[3]

• • •

After imagining something new and shaping a new ordinary around it, the biggest challenge is to repeat the process over time. How can we ensure that our business can imagine, explore, and create new scripts, while running existing operations?

This chapter will examine this skill of mental ambidexterity, look at actions for sustaining imagination alongside execution, blocks to doing so, a useful game, questions to ask, and a diagnostic.

What Is Mental Ambidexterity?

Many have written about the physical side of ambidexterity in business, meaning organizing a company to do two things at once: explore new opportunities and exploit existing ones.[4] Yet there is an important mental side to this as well. The mental challenge is to keep imagination active over time, within and beyond the scripted corporate models that we build when institutionalizing an idea. Thinking of a company as a connected set of brains orchestrating resources, how can these brains handle the factual and the counterfactual worlds at the same time and across time? What is required mentally to pursue two contrasting directions at once: explore and exploit, rethink and optimize, imagine and execute?

Amazon's first website (1995) and an AI-powered Amazon Go store (2020).
Source: Courtesy of Amazon.

Imagination becomes particularly difficult to sustain in well-established companies, where the need to reinvent may not be immediately apparent. Many executives worry about this dark side of growth and success. We conducted a cross-industry survey of 136 large companies, including 55 C-suite executives, and 97 percent said that imagination was critically important for business, although 80 percent thought that imagination was hard to realize in large companies.[5] Andre Haddad, CEO of car-sharing company Turo, described to

us the difficulty of keeping imagination alive, even in a relatively young company:

> It's my number-one worry. We are at a stage now where we are adding more and more people. They are very capable, very smart, they are a good cultural fit. But they are coming now when the company has a lot of things figured out already—customer support, insurance, marketing, data management . . . There's a

way that exists. And that way is correlated with success to date. So there is an attitude which is: "I've got to learn this way and adapt to it, maybe find ways to preserve it, or, not screw up anything that's already working." I think that attitude is not the attitude the team had back in 2010.[6]

The core problem is that the imagining and executing mindsets don't naturally fit together—in fact, they are often antagonistic. Emphasizing one has the potential to undermine the other. (See table 8-1.)

Both mindsets are important to a successful company. If we focus on execution and efficiency alone, the company becomes oriented around financial metrics. Opportunities, in the form of early-stage imaginative ideas, appear as unevidenced and speculative. On the other hand, if we focus only on imagination, we don't commit to a model for long enough to realize all its value. The all-imagination company tends not to survive for long. There are many established companies of the all-execution type that have atrophied the ability to foster new ideas.

How to Sustain Imagination

There are four routes to supporting mental ambidexterity to sustain imagination alongside operational efficiency: supporting imagination in everyone, in some people, in teams, or in an external business ecosystem. Below we explore actions

Table 8-1 Imagination-focused versus execution-focused thinking

Imagination-focused thinking	Execution-focused thinking
Counterfactual	Factual
Challenges existing models	Uses existing models
Speculative	Evidence- and measurement-based
Tricky to communicate	Easy to communicate
Unpredictable timeline	Constrained by deadlines
Future value	Immediate value
Effectiveness	Efficiency

. . . And this is where we keep those accused of imagination and free thinking . . .

The Renaissance Mind

We want to turn business people into Renaissance people in order to open up their imaginative faculties . . . So what can we do? I think we need to scale back the functionalism and mono-dimensional nature of how we educate people into being corporate men and women.

—Claus Dierksmeier, philosopher, Chair for Globalization Ethics, University of Tübingen

The Renaissance gives us a stellar example of the execution mindset and the imagination mindset combined. The reason we have the idea of the "Renaissance man" is that figures of the Renaissance were less specialized than people today. One might be interested simultaneously in geography, botany, military studies, government administration, poetry, and so on. From a business perspective, these areas are not necessarily directly useful in themselves, but they provide someone with a rich set of mental models to draw on.

Johann Wolfgang von Goethe, often called the last figure of the Renaissance, had the kind of mind that we are seeking to cultivate. He liked to refer to the albatross, which flies around magnificently in the air (symbolizing exploring the heights of imagination), but flounders when trying to walk on the deck of a ship.[a] Goethe wanted to do both well; to be both excellent at imagination and a pragmatic executor. He acted out this Renaissance philosophy in his life: he wrote Europe's first bestseller novel, *The Sorrows of Young Werther,* and was also a diligent minister for mines and roads in the Dutchy of Weimar; he created *Faust* and organized recruiting for the Prussian military; he had amorous adventures in Italy and also wrote about "the beauty of double-entry book-keeping." Goethe portrays his core worldview in a novel, *Wilhelm Meister's Apprenticeship*, in which the artistic mindset and the commercial mindset start out opposed in the protagonist's life but end up intertwined and supporting each other.

This ideal of the Renaissance mind persisted until the Romantic period in the eighteenth and nineteenth centuries. The Romantics contributed to undermining the goal of well-roundedness, which had permeated liberal arts education; instead, they emphasized erratic artistic genius and a choice between soulless commerce and spiritual art. Influential Romantic thinkers contrasted themselves with bureaucrats, who they portrayed as obsessed by process and quantification, being uninspired and unwilling to rethink.[b] The Romantics are the predecessors of the figure of the disgruntled imaginative person who can't find a home in a corporation, and who blames the corporation or capitalism. Indeed, the Romantics made being disgruntled heroic: the tragic genius. Instead, what *should* be heroic is seeking to be both a pragmatic businessperson *and* an imaginative person.

Goethe does not have to be the last Renaissance mind. We can bring together the mindsets of imagination and execution, as individual business leaders and also as collections of minds in teams, companies, and business ecosystems.

NOTES

a. J. Armstrong, *Love, Life, Goethe: How to Be Happy in an Imperfect World* (London: Penguin, 2006).

b. I. Berlin, *The Roots of Romanticism* (Princeton, NJ: Princeton University Press, 2013).

along each of these paths that a business can take to sustain imagination over time.

In Everyone

One route to sustaining imagination is to adopt policies that trigger and support imagination for everyone in the company—aiming for every individual to be mentally ambidextrous, at least to some degree.

MAINTAIN NOVEL INFORMATION FLOWS

A company can sustain imagination by shaping the information that people are exposed to in order to maximize contact with the outside and with otherness, promoting surprise and rethinking. We don't often reflect on how information is delivered and consumed across an entire company, but we can be more deliberate about it.

Jared Cohen, CEO of Jigsaw, sees his role as a leader as exposing his staff to things that will inspire them. One policy Jigsaw has adopted is to bring users of its products and services into the office to spend time with employees and to trigger them to imagine new services. As Cohen said to us, "There has to be some inspiration from the founder, but if we are relying on me only for this, that's not going to work. My job is to expose them to things that will inspire them. So we bring in people like investigative journalists from Russia, or activists from Zimbabwe, to come spend a month. We have a program for this and we call them 'users in residence.'"[7]

The point here is to expose people in the company to things not immediately relevant to the task at hand, but that (at least sometimes) will prompt them to reimagine aspects of the business. This also counteracts a company's tendency to focus internally as it grows larger.

Another example of systematically sustaining imagination is Takeda Pharmaceuticals. Believing that it could not sustain innovation without maintaining individual curiosity, it built the Center for Scientific Leadership and Innovation, based on the principles of "four Cs": collaborative networks, collective intelligence, focused curiosity, and creative energy. The center invites outside speakers to discuss the topic of curiosity and imagination, codifies best practices for collective learning and works with project teams to bring them to life.

Other ways we can maintain novel information flows include sending employees to industry conferences, particularly those of *other* industries, where they might have their imagination triggered. Another more radical idea is to create an AI-driven system that provides a tailored tasting menu of information for each employee every day, to help them develop new mental models across diverse fields of thought. We all have information feeds (the websites we visit in the morning, the lists we've subscribed to, and so on), but we generally don't design them specifically to maximize surprise. Such a system would be something like Amazon's recommendation engine, but rather than "show me something I will like," the aim would be to "show me something unfamiliar but imagination-provoking." The algorithm could be personalized based on an understanding of a person's most familiar mental models and thus the kinds of information

Oh—the new CEO thinks it helps keep us inspired.

that might best provoke surprise, refined with constant feedback.

ATTRACT AND DEVELOP IMAGINATION SKILLS

Another way to sustain imagination across everyone in the company is to attract, cultivate, and recognize the constituent skills of imagination. This requires identifying and cultivating a different kind of talent in both hiring and promotion. We can look across each of the areas covered in this book, identify the underlying skills relating to each and reflect this in criteria for hiring and promotion:

- Ability to see and care about surprise

  - The skill of focusing on and analyzing anomalies. Assess this criterion by presenting scenarios or datasets to see if the person picks up on anomalies.

  - The ability to use analogies. Test for this as part of a case study problem, asking, "What analogies could be useful here?"

- Ability to rethink mental models

  - Having cognitive diversity within one mind: a range of mental models from different disciplines and practices.

  - The ability to take multiple perspectives on a topic, that is, the skill of keeping multiple mental models in mind.

- Willingness and ability to collide ideas with the world

  - The sense of playfulness: the skills of improvising and following hunches confidently.

  - Willingness to experiment. To test for this, ask about the person's history of experimenting: when they tried out a new idea or how often they fully realized their ideas.

- Ability to broker across groups to cultivate collective imagination

  - The skills of being an idea broker between mindsets and groups.

  - Ability to use stories effectively. Test this by giving the person a new imaginative mental model and asking them to illustrate it with a story.

- Ability to turn ideas into institutional scripts

  - The skill of analyzing and articulating the essence of why an imaginative experiment worked.

  - The skill of articulating clear and useful rules. Test this by asking the individual to define rules or principles to operationalize a novel idea.

- The capacity for serial imagination

  - Having a track record of pursuing and leading journeys of imagination: rethinking mental models, acting on them, involving others, and turning successful experiments into institutional scripts.

DESIGN FOR REFLECTION

Another way to sustain imagination is to design spaces and schedules across the company to support reflection and rethinking. Usually, when a business aims to design for imagination and creativity, the template consists of bright colors and architecture that breaks rules.

But as Polish architect Magdalena Priefer told us:

> Another important point is overstimulation. Some creative office spaces seem to emphasize with every element that being creative and inventive is the most important goal for people working there. That kind of approach can be very stressful and frustrating, and paradoxically, it can block or limit the imagination. Often spaces like those are also overloading with sensory stimuli, which is tiring and weakens imagination. An optimal workplace should stimulate (without overloading), inspire, intrigue, and give freedom of choice.[8]

The visual environment is linked closely to our physiological responses. In spaces with few elements, which are easier to process, pulse rate and blood pressure decrease, in contrast to spaces that are visually busy.[9] Visually busy spaces play more to our sympathetic, fight-or-flight system, than to our parasympathetic, rest-and-digest system which supports reflection.[10] We should seek to create spaces of tranquility that support rethinking of our mental models.

We should also design the use of time to permit and encourage reflection and rethinking. Employees could schedule

A space designed to stimulate reflection and rethinking. *Source:* Courtesy of Magdalena Priefer.

an hour or two per day specifically for low-input time, which they could record on official time sheets—time to momentarily put aside what is urgent, for what is long term and important: exploring the counterfactual. When we walk into an office and 25 percent of people are staring out the window, that is not necessarily a bad thing. It could be a sign of brains being used well.

ALLOW ROLE FLEXIBILITY

Another policy for keeping imagination alive in everyone in a company is to enable and encourage flexibility in roles. The challenge is to create the mindset that everyone can, and even has the obligation to, pursue an imaginative idea, even if it takes them outside the preset scope of work.

Many established companies create pressure for people *not* to act outside given roles. Each role has a defined job to be done, with promotion and monetary rewards tied to that being accomplished. Yet this can reduce openness to considering accidents and anomalies, and narrow the scope for developing and trying out counterfactual mental models.

Recruit Holdings aims to counteract this by communicating to new hires and existing employees that the entire company is a work in progress—that it belongs to employees in the sense that they can contribute to its development. One rationale behind Recruit's annual festival of ideas is to encourage the audience to step beyond their prescribed corporate roles to develop new ideas. A leader of this effort, Takanori Makiguchi, told us, "One of the main reasons for the FORUM is to lower the barriers to doing something new, to send 'you can do this too' signals."[11]

Ed Catmull, founder of Pixar, discusses how he aims to instill a similar mindset:

> The bigger issue for us has been getting young new hires to have the confidence to speak up. To try to remedy this, I make it a practice to speak at the orientation sessions for new hires, where I talk about the mistakes we've made and the lessons we've learned. My intent is to persuade them that we haven't gotten it all figured out and that we want everyone to question why we're doing something that doesn't seem to make sense to them. We do not want people to assume that because we are successful, everything we do is right.[12]

As a business leader, you can use your position to communicate this point: that the company is a work in progress, and the roles and rules it sets are parts of an evolving script, not immutable laws. Amazon has a principle within a list of "Leadership Principles" that explicitly tells people to act beyond their roles: "Leaders are owners . . . They act on behalf of the entire company, beyond just their own team. They never say 'that's not my job.'"[13]

In Some People

Getting *everyone* in a company to be imaginative is a nice goal but is not always attainable. A more realistic goal may be to cultivate imagination in some people, who help sustain imagination for the company as a whole.

PROTECT MAVERICKS

Individuals with a tendency toward imagination often need protecting in a firm. Their eclectic contacts and stock of perspectives may not be valued by people whose minds are entrenched in one area or one best way of doing things; indeed, their constant development and spreading of new ideas can be regarded as heresy or threat.

When we asked Carl Stern, a former CEO of BCG, what were the most impactful things he did as a leader that were least visible, he explained that one of his most important jobs as CEO was "to protect mavericks," those individuals who exist on the periphery or in the interstices of an organization who originate and share ideas. He added, "Mavericks tend to be a pain in the ass to manage and middle managers will therefore often try to kill them."[14]

I think the captain is taking the concept of fluidity of roles way too far.

Simon is such an original thinker!

One policy for supporting some people in being imaginative is to establish multiple paths to success. At BCG, we have a generalist consulting career track as well as an expert track for people who want to develop deep specialized knowledge. A company could go further and develop an imaginative track, which is something we have attempted to do at the BCG Henderson Institute by setting up a fellows program, allowing thought leaders within BCG to set aside 30 percent of their time for a period of three years to rethink an important aspect of business.

SELF-DISRUPT

Another way of sustaining imagination by cultivating it in some people is to direct a group of people to focus on disrupting the business. The rationale for self-disruption is that in an established business, mental models tend to become entrenched. The core business model shapes habits, roles, and expectations, which can become a self-sustaining system. The dominant business logic comes to seem like the way the world really is. As philosopher John Armstrong notes: "Commonsense—what one is supposed to think about how things really are—is often itself a mental model that is carrying all kinds of burdens, involves exaggerations and omissions, and can be very distorted. But because of the consensus around it, among certain sorts of people, it passes for how things actually are."[15] A company must therefore work to actively create space for internal doubt of its current business model and the mental model behind it. Space for doubt means space for imaginative rethinking.

One way to do this is to have an imaginative person be a dissenting voice or devil's advocate at key meetings. For any key project or decision, have someone think through a different and even contradictory mental model from the one in use and present that alongside the normal approach. This idea derives from the policies of the Catholic Church in the sixteenth century, then the largest bureaucracy of its day. It invented the position *advocatus diaboli*, advocate of the devil, who would argue the opposing side when the hierarchy was discussing who to canonize.[16] When this person did their job *well*, they brought up a compelling position counter to the prevailing view. In business we could learn from this by insisting that business cases should not be discussed without there being a credible, well-articulated alternative.

Another tactic is to create a few teams focused on disrupting the business. Our default approach here is to have an

R&D department, which is supposed to do all the envisioning and radical thinking. But it is possible to usefully disrupt the business more directly, in parallel to running it. PepsiCo's soft drinks business, for example, is divided between those working on getting the most out of the current bottled and canned drinks, and those developing in-home carbonation machines, which, if successful, will cannibalize sales of the former. This may seem destructive. However, if PepsiCo did not think imaginatively and disrupt itself, competitors would likely do so. As former CEO Indra Nooyi describes it, "In each business we have two strands: the day-to-day group, and the future group, thinking, 'How do I disrupt myself?' The team that runs the core business should keep doing what they're doing efficiently: worrying about the cost per pound to the decimal. The other team should not be motivated by the current model and should focus totally on disrupting it."[17]

But Jimmy, we have everything we need here . . .

In Teams

Another way to sustain imagination across a business, rather than trying to cultivate it in everyone or in only a minority of people, is to ensure every *team* across the company is equipped with this capacity. That is, to make each team ambidextrous with respect to imagination and efficiency.

BUILD COGNITIVE DIVERSITY

One way to achieve this is by building cognitive diversity into every team. Joint research by BCG and AI-neuroscience based startup pymetrics shows that large companies need cognitive diversity in order to cope with complex and dynamic business environments.[18] We can identify three strands of cognitive diversity:

- *Diversity in personality.* Genetic temperament and personal formative history, which together shape dispositions, tendencies, and capacities.

- *Diversity in styles of thinking.* Variations in attention, effort, decision making, resilience, generosity, learning, and risk tolerance, which influence the ability to solve different types of problem.

- *Diversity in mental models.* Variety in the stock of mental models drawn from different disciplines, worldviews, professional experiences, and so on.

Cognitive diversity is often entwined with other forms of diversity; one reason that involving a range of ethnic and cultural backgrounds is good is that different life experiences often give rise to helpfully different perspectives. Building each of these three strands of cognitive diversity into teams will help them be collectively ambidextrous. On the one hand, cognitive diversity helps with execution—by involving personalities, styles of thinking, and mental models oriented around analyzing and managing "what is." On the other hand, cognitive diversity also underpins imagination—by ensuring a wide stock of mental models to trigger surprise and mine analogies from, as well as providing a diversity of personalities and thinking styles for a mental model to pass through as it evolves.

SET UP TRADING ZONES

To use diversity in teams, we need to ensure that people with different personalities, thinking styles, and perspectives are able to communicate effectively with each other. This is difficult because people with different ways of seeing and processing the world often struggle to communicate smoothly with each other. It can be hard to create sympathy and conversation between those who want to manage the corporate machine and those who want to rethink and disrupt it.

We can learn from the concept of trading zones, as defined in anthropology. A trading zone is a place where different cultures meet and do business, such as the great historical trading ports of Venice, Italy, or Dubrovnik, Croatia. Trading zones can also occur within intellectual disciplines. Historian Peter Galison studied how trading zones in physics worked across communities in the last century. He found that theoreticians, experimental physicists, and engineers had distinct and often mutually wary subcultures, similar to different groups within a corporation. But they could work together by developing practices of "local coordination": listening, seeking to translate their concepts carefully for other groups, and focusing on the areas where they could have mutually interesting conversations.[19]

At the BCG Henderson Institute, we have a number of initiatives that aim to foster close interactions between different types of minds. One example is our annual "Meeting of Minds" discussion we host in New York or San Francisco. We identify core problems companies will be dealing with in the next five years and bring imaginative thinkers from diverse fields (biology, political science, mathematics, cognitive science) together with business leaders (CEOs, chief innovation officers, BCG partners) for a discussion. Throughout the year we also host a series of dinners that bring together scientists and business leaders. During these efforts, we have developed some principles to make such meetings flow, which can be applied more broadly to building mixed imagination-execution teams in business:

- Have lots of interpersonal engagement, mixing discussions and joint activity to build mutual knowledge and trust.

- Set big topics of common interest to spark engagement.

- Use plain language rather than field-specific jargon.

- Allow discussions to evolve naturally.

- Emphasize openness and listening over the desire to prove oneself—and choose participants accordingly.

- Make a feature of and celebrate the diversity of the group.

- Tie the meeting to a collective effort like the joint creation of an article.

In an Ecosystem

To sustain imagination, we can look beyond the company as well. We can design our company to draw on the capacity

for imagination and the products of imagination from customers and other companies within a broader business ecosystem.

BUILD AN ECOSYSTEM

We define a business ecosystem as "a dynamic group of largely independent economic players that create products or services that together constitute a coherent solution."[20] There are two broad kinds of ecosystem we can build, both of which draw on the imaginations of others in different ways.

The first is a solution ecosystem in which a core firm orchestrates the offering of several complementor firms to create a product or service, for example, all the firms that contribute to a PC. In the 1980s and 1990s, Intel built an effective ecosystem: it not only sold microchips, it swapped intellectual property and ideas with a range of other companies contributing to the PC, to expand the functionality of computers and thus expand its overall market. Intel created networks of collective imagination that went beyond its company to encompass businesses developing broadband, graphics, security, the USB, and DVDs.[21] Like Intel, then, one option for sustaining imagination is to bring together an ecosystem of companies, which mutually draw on each other's imaginative and other capacities for mutual benefit.

The second kind of ecosystem is a transaction ecosystem in which a central platform connects third-party products or services with customers. For example, Amazon draws on third-party sellers who imagine and make products that then become part of Amazon's offering as a whole. (Incidentally,

at the time, many people within Amazon resisted this counterfactual idea: to invite third parties in and increase competition with the firm's own offerings.[22]) Airbnb is another example. Unlike a hotel chain, the company does not have to imagine and reimagine its entire offering. Its hosts do this, by creating an ever-evolving portfolio of accommodation options. Airbnb itself rethinks the tools it offers to hosts, but it expands its imaginative output as a company by facilitating the imaginations of all the hosts within its ecosystem. To sustain imagination alongside execution, therefore, another option is to develop a platform that attracts, supports, and markets the imaginative productions of others.

Blocks to Sustaining Imagination

There are a number of blocks that get in the way of efforts to sustain imaginative thinking alongside the execution-focused mindset across a business.

Overspecialization

This block is created by employees becoming laser-focused on their own particular domain to the point that different subcultures and jargon develop. This makes it hard for people reimagining things to talk to the people who will execute those things: specialized groups are more likely to be wary of outsiders, and the jargon creates a barrier. The solution: move people around the company often so they experience many different functions and roles and the mental models underpinning each, cross-fertilizing these different perspectives in the process.

Insularity

This pathology is created by being unwilling or unable to look outside the company to encounter surprise and draw on the imaginations of others. It could be caused by fear of losing control (customers and third-party businesses can't be instructed in the ways employees can) or by defining roles using an entirely internal logic. The antidote is to ensure that a proportion of everyone's time and attention is focused on external matters.

Kafka Syndrome

In Franz Kafka's novel *The Trial*, one person is beaten down by a large, confusing organization according to processes

New Metrics

However a business achieves mental ambidexterity, it will need to measure and reward the right things to sustain this. Most metrics that businesses use to measure success are based on what has happened in the past: growth, market share, profitability, and so on. The implicit assumption is that past performance is likely to persist into the future. However, as we saw earlier in the book, this assumption is becoming less tenable. A company measuring only past-value capture will systematically underestimate and therefore neglect the value of new ideas.

When we seek to understand a person, we look at what they have done and been in the past. But we also instinctually make an effort to consider their future possibilities and potential. In business, although hard data will by definition come from past events, we should try to consider fitness for the future as well, using different types of indicators.

- Measuring imaginative capacity directly. Based on the skills assessment outlined in this chapter in the section on attracting and developing imagination skills, a firm could create a measure of imaginative capacity across its members.

- More indirect measures of imagination focusing downstream on innovation output. For example, a freshness

index of the share of offerings or sales which incorporate recent innovations.

- Measuring enterprise vitality, which we define as the capacity to reinvent the business and grow sustainably. This measurement might draw on numerous kinds of financial and nonfinancial data which predict forward-looking innovation and growth, as opposed to reporting past performance.[a]

NOTE

a. Martin Reeves et al., "Measuring and Managing Corporate Vitality," BCG, October 19, 2017, https://www.bcg.com/publications/2017/strategy-strategic -planning-measuring-managing-corporate-vitality.

that are never explained (in German, it was appropriately called *Der Process*). This probably resonates for many of us. In the layers of hierarchy in large corporations, we tend to lose a sense of our own agency. For example, we might wish that we had a wider range of sandwiches at the cafeteria, but because this is not our responsibility, no one working in the cafeteria is directly responsible, and it is unclear who makes the decision anyway, it feels pointless to even try. Why bother imagining how things could be different? This feeling is the Kafka syndrome, a block to imagination. One solution, ironically, is to add another process: a way to register aggravations, aspirations, and early-stage ideas that is linked to funding opportunities and decision-making capacity.

Resignation

Recently, one of the authors flew on an airline in the United States. His assigned seat was broken. When he pointed this out, "Excuse me, this is broken," the response from the flight attendant was, "Well, what do you think it's like to *work* here?" We can take this comment as symbolizing a final stage of corporate decline: if the sense of resignation spreads far enough, no one sees the point in seeing, caring, or imagining. One countermeasure is to focus on helping mavericks: give them more power to implement new and inspiring initiatives and help others feel that they could contribute in the same way.

Success Trap

This block to sustaining imagination comes from the assumption that the way the company was when it achieved success must be the apex of its evolution. In the words of BCG's founder Bruce Henderson, "Success in the past always becomes enshrined in the present by the over-valuation of the policies and attitudes which accompanied that success."[23] The collective imagination of a firm may be dying, but the general atmosphere of success and backward-looking performance indicators prevent people seeing how the organization could be reimagined and transformed for *future* success. The countermeasure is to follow Amazon's Day 1 philosophy: keep alive the sense that the company could go in any direction from here, that journeys of imagination and growth are always ahead. Another approach is to look at forward-looking metrics to assess the business's growth potential.

So, who wants these leaves anyway?

I dunno, mate—I just work here.

A Game to Play

The Destroy Your Business Game

To keep imagination alive and prompt ideas about reimagining your own company, a useful game is to imagine how your company could lose to disruptors.

Select an area of your business and contemplate how to disrupt it. List the key disruptors that are implicitly making bets against your business model. For example, a real estate company might identify a range of smaller startups seeking to reimagine how people buy and sell houses. Reduce this range of bets to a few clusters of similar bets. For instance, there might be a few startups betting on entirely removing the real estate agent from the process, another group adding in a range of additional services, and so on.

Imagine each kind of bet becoming successful. The key is not to ask whether the bet *will* be successful, but rather, *if it were*, what would happen and what would be the consequences. For example, the real estate firm might consider the disruptor Redfin, an app that does not use estate agents.

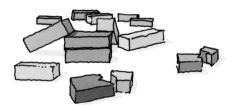

One can picture a future in which Redfin, currently small, becomes a $5 billion firm, and most houses are bought and sold via its app. Imagine, step by step, how the disruptor overtook your business. What strategic moves did it make? What capabilities did it develop or acquire? What were the dynamics of people's preferences, technology, and the blocks within your own business that led to Redfin's efforts being more successful than yours?

General Electric systematized this approach in the 1990s, asking each of its units to have one "DestroyYourBusiness.com" team to come up with internet-based disruptive ideas.[24] The exercise surfaces your company's vulnerabilities and identifies disruptors' potential moves and success factors. Once you have identified these, you can consider if any of them trigger new ways to imagine your current company.

Good Questions to Ask

Some good questions to ask when trying to sustain the imaginative capacity of your organization are:

- What was the entrepreneurial vision on which the firm was founded?

- How can we recreate that spirit today?

- What is the next big idea that will drive the growth of the firm?

- What are the obstacles to such ideas coming forward and being developed?

- All organizations will eventually fail. How might ours fail? Having considered that, what can we do about it?

- If we were founding the business today and all options were feasible, which path of growth would we pursue?

- Are we recruiting for, cultivating, and recognizing skills of imagination? How could we do this better?

- Is the firm fully tapping into entrepreneurial talent internally and externally?

Organizational Diagnostic

This diagnostic tool assesses your organization's capacity to sustain imagination. Each question is linked to a related action in this chapter. If you score low on a particular area, refer back to that action in the chapter.

		Never (1)	Rarely or less than once a year (2)	Sometimes or once a month to once a year (3)	Usually or once a week to once a month (4)	Always or more often than weekly (5)
	Related action					
Our business supplies employees with thought-provoking information from nonbusiness worldviews (e.g., history, science, literature) through lectures, training, or articles.	Maintain novel information flows					
Hiring, promotions, and rewards take the capacity for imagination into account.	Attract and develop imagination skills					
The firm has a range of quiet, less stimulating physical spaces to support reflection and rethinking.	Design for reflection					
Employees feel that the business is a work in progress and they can contribute to its evolution.	Allow role flexibility					
It is normal for employees to voice dissenting opinions or challenge aspects of the current business model.	Self-disrupt					
We have forums to exchange ideas across departments or with external thinkers.	Set up trading zones					
Our company actively engages and draws on ideas from people beyond the firm.	Build an ecosystem					
Our business uses metrics linked to imagination or reinvention.	New metrics (see the sidebar)					
TOTAL						

After you have added up your total, score your current situation: 31–35, excellent; 21–30, good; 11–20, moderate; 0–10, poor. To benchmark your score against other organizations, please visit www.theimaginationmachine.org.

Chapter Nine

ARTIFICIAL IMAGINATION?

Can machines imagine? The way we normally think about computers is that they take instructions we give them, calculate, and produce a result. We don't think of computers as having imagination as we have defined it: getting surprised, developing counterfactual models, and exploring the new possibilities. Yet Blaise Agüera y Arcas, distinguished scientist at Google AI, has pushed the boundaries of computation, creating algorithms that do surprisingly imaginative things. (See figure 9-1.)

Agüera y Arcas and his team trained an algorithm to recognize birds and then prompted it to create new pictures based on its understanding of birds. When we interviewed him, we asked how this relates to imagination. As he put it, the AI is exploring a "manifold": the space of all possible things that we might still call a bird, similar to how imagination explores nonabsurd counterfactual possibilities. "These neural nets are finding manifolds of stuff they have been trained on, and they can wander through that manifold and generate plausible things."[1]

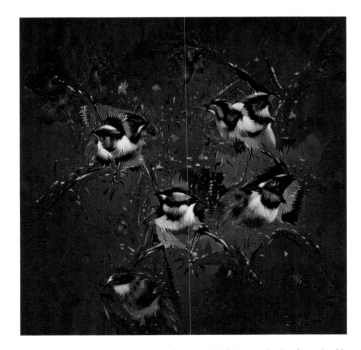

Figure 9-1 A somewhat surreal picture of birds made by Google AI

Source: Courtesy of Michael Tyka.

Such recent developments in AI, which appear to be encroaching on territory we have described as imagination, raise the question of whether the model of human imagination underpinning this book is but a temporary one—whether computers will eventually substitute for humans in the realm of imagination too.

• • •

The use of AI for *routine* cognitive tasks is one of the motivations for this book: as machines develop cognitively, we need to get more systematic about understanding and harnessing our unique human capacities, especially imagination. As AI continues to progress, however, it challenges the idea that imagination will always be unique to humans. Will humans eventually be replaced in this area too? Can AI help us to imagine? And what can AI teach us about imagination and how to harness it in business?

Will We Be Replaced?

Some outputs from today's AI seem to come from the imagination. Does this mean that AI will replace our imaginations? Let's look at a few examples before answering this question.

Artist Mario Klingemann prompted the AI known as Generative Pretrained Transformer 3 (GTP-3) to write a story about Twitter in the style of English satirical author Jerome K. Jerome. The only input he gave it was the title, the author's name, and the first word of the story. What the AI wrote could plausibly have come from a human mind: "It is a curious fact that the last remaining form of social life in which the people of London are still interested is Twitter. I was struck with this curious fact when I went on one of my periodical holidays to the sea-side, and found the whole place twittering like a starling-cage."[2]

To take a less literary example, the same AI was prompted to write something with a more practical focus: an essay on possible startups on Mars:

> Here's the sort of startup that might make a go of it on Mars: one that makes money by taking advantage of local resources. For example, a startup that uses the Martian atmosphere to make fertilizer or methane fuel. A startup that sells water from Martian rivers. A startup that uses minerals from the Martian soil. A startup that uses solar power from the Martian sun. A startup that uses a new kind of solar panel that's more efficient at converting sunlight into electricity.
>
> I would even invest in a startup that did nothing but extract the helium-3 from the Martian atmosphere and send it back to Earth.[3]

AI has also been used to create new things in the world beyond clever writing. In 2019, design and communications company AKQA used AI to create a new sport. It trained an algorithm on the rules of four hundred sports, from which it produced a thousand new ideas for games. Many were absurd, but the team narrowed down the list to ten and then field-tested three. From this, it picked one, which the computer had named "Speedgate" (see figure 9-2).

Some aspects of the game are familiar, but overall it is strikingly original. Speedgate is played with a rugby-like ball, which players can pass and kick. Each team must kick the ball through the center posts to unlock their ability to score at the end posts. Scoring through the end posts (from either direction) is worth two points, and if one of the players catches the ball when it is kicked through and kicks it back, the score is upgraded to three.

The company practiced playing Speedgate, developed a campaign to publicize it, and helped found Speedgate leagues. There are now teams around the world; AKQA describes it as "the world's first sport imagined by AI."[4]

This example seems to show artificial imagination: the machine generated new ideas, one of which has gone from being counterfactual to becoming a valued addition to the world. This has occurred in other areas as well. In 2017, a teenager from West Virginia wrote an algorithm to write rap lyrics. Three students in Paris took the code, tweaked it, and applied it to paintings. They selected a few outputs, one of which, named *Edmond de Belamy*, was sold at a Christie's auction in 2018 for $432,500 (see figure 9-3).[5] The painting is signed using a section of the algorithm's code:

$$\min_{G} \max_{D} \mathrm{E}_x \left[\log(D(x)) \right] + \mathrm{E}_z \left[\log(1 - D(G(z))) \right]$$

AI is also beginning to routinely execute activities in business that it would be natural to call "creative." Companies

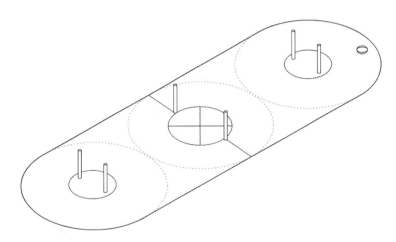

Figure 9-2 Playing the AI-created sport Speedgate (top) and the AI-designed field (bottom)

Source: Courtesy of AKQA.

Figure 9-3 *Edmond de Belamy*, **an AI-generated painting**
Source: Courtesy of OBVIOUS.

your style from a wide variety of colors ranging from timeless black, blue, and grey, to bold red and orange. With jeans available in waist sizes from 28 to 60, find the one that matches your exact needs. To ensure your satisfaction, [company] carries roughly 120 items earning a 4-star rating or better. With prices below $100, get incredible deals on top brands including Levi's, Lee, Dickies, Wrangler, and more. With 212 options available online and 86 more ready for in-store pickup, [company] is confident you can find exactly what you need for your next occasion.[6]

Natural-language generation tools are also used to create marketing content tailored to individual customers.[7] In journalism, Bloomberg has an AI, "Cyborg," which creates first drafts of articles by drawing on financial reports. And the *Washington Post* used its algorithm "Heliograf" to create 850 published stories over a year.[8]

AI is also being used in pharmacology to find novel molecules to fight fibrosis and cancer.[9] We may be less likely to think of inventing drugs as imaginative work, compared to say inventing sports or making paintings, but the underlying achievement is the same. The AI picked out valuable options from a vast space of unrealized—counterfactual—possibilities.

What can we conclude from these examples? Software is making remarkable strides in producing outputs that look like human creative outputs, in some cases with significant monetary value. So the boundary between humans and machines is certainly shifting, and we should expect this to continue.

such as Automated Insights are using AI to create draft narratives around different products, such as this text written by AI about jeans:

> Regardless of the circumstance, [company]'s impressive selection of men's jeans is sure to have something for you. Whether you prefer relaxed, slim, or classic fit, [company] has you covered. Pick the one that fits

I think our AI just beat yours, so the war is over.

words. What it does is something like a massive act of cutting and pasting, stitching variations on text that it has seen, rather than digging deeply for the concepts that underlie those texts."[11]

AI also lacks another fundamental part of imagination: a motive to imagine. The motive is not just the impetus for starting the process, it is a guide for what a particular imaginative process should be about—what is important to rethink.

Neither does AI connect words to the world. As philosopher David Chalmers writes, GPT-3 "does many things that would require understanding in humans, but it never really connects its words to perception and action."[12] As we have seen, imagination not connected with refocusing, moving in the world, experimenting, or communicating is mere private reverie. In the examples given of sports, art, and journalism, humans supplied this bridging role between computation and the real world.

We can conclude that without a causal model, connection to perception and action, or any aspirations or frustrations other than those given to them by people, AI will not be replacing human imagination any time soon.

What we have seen, however, is that the products of AI can be valuable in generating grist for thought; humans can develop machine outputs into a usable result. This suggests a different perspective, which Agüera y Arcas of Google emphasized to us: "You have to problematize the idea that AI is separate from humanity. If you zoom out and look at the bigger socio-technical system, AI is just another human expression. It's part of this whole, giant machine, made up of humans combined with everything they have invented."[13]

However, computers are still far from possessing certain capacities that are fundamental to imagination. The first is having a causal mental model. GPT-3 is a neural network that has been exposed to a huge amount of data from the internet and books (the 6 million articles of Wikipedia made up only 0.6 percent of its training data).[10] On the surface, this seems similar to what we have been talking about in this book: a mental model, informed by the world, which can generate nonabsurd novelty.

But GPT-3 is a *language* model; it only represents the probability of one string of text following another. AI researchers Gary Marcus and Ernest Davis observe of systems like GPT-3: "They don't learn about the world—they learn about text and how people use words in relation to other

Rather than whether we will be replaced, then, the more relevant question perhaps is how this colossal collaboration will evolve. What are the ways AI might work with us and enhance our imaginative capability?

Can AI Help Us Imagine?

For an overall view of the different possibilities for human-AI collaboration, we can use the framework that computer scientist and businessman Kai-Fu Lee presents in his book *AI Superpowers* (see figure 9-4).

The horizontal axis maps roles requiring more efficiency (exploiting something known) versus roles requiring more imagination (exploring the possible). The vertical axis maps empathizing (recognizing and responding to the mental states of others) versus systematizing (working with or building a rules-based system).[14] Figure 9-5 shows this framework populated with particular roles.

In the lower-left quadrant are roles focused around working efficiently within rules-based systems, such as a truck driver, cook, accountant, mechanic, or market analyst. AI is likely to largely take over such roles. In the upper-left quadrant are roles requiring empathy in well-known territory, such as a nurse, retail salesperson, journalist, or general physician. These roles will have AI involved in core operations, but humans will still interpret outputs and interface with people; for example, sports journalism created by AI but tweaked by a human, or a physician who relies largely on AI for analysis and focuses on compassionate engagement with the patient.

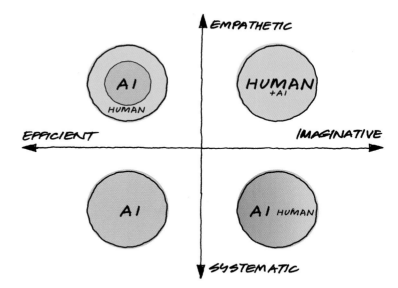

Figure 9-4 Different kinds of AI-human collaboration

Source: Adapted from Kai-Fu Lee, *AI Superpowers: China, Silicon Valley, and the New World Order* (New York: Houghton Mifflin Harcourt, 2018). Reproduced by permission of the author.

In the lower-right quadrant are roles that work with rules-based systems but that require counterfactual thinking, such as programmer, engineer, event planner, or soldier. These will become an extensive human-AI collaboration on imagination, such as a graphic designer who works with AI tools, playing them like a musician plays an instrument, or a soldier whose informational world is shaped by AI while dealing with unexpected situations. Finally, in the upper-right quadrant are roles that depend heavily on reading others correctly, as well as imagination—for creating new things, responding to unique situations, or exploring what the future might be. These roles

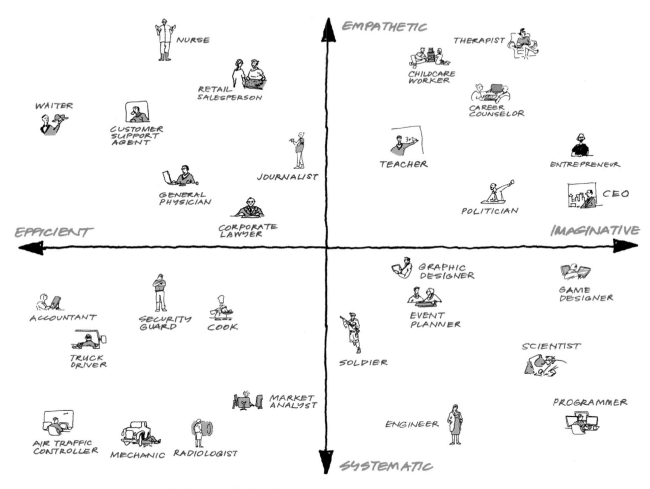

Figure 9-5 Particular roles in AI-human collaboration

Source: Adapted from Kai-Fu Lee, *AI Superpowers: China, Silicon Valley, and the New World Order* (New York: Houghton Mifflin Harcourt, 2018). Reproduced by permission of the author.

will remain largely human-directed, with some AI support, such as therapist or life coach, politician, CEO, or entrepreneur.

From this matrix, we can see that AI can work with humans in a few ways. AI can free us from more routine activities; it can carry out core tasks, to which humans bring a layer of empathy; or it can provide an ongoing stimulus for imagination. We can speculate how different kinds of AI-human collaboration might play out across each of the areas examined in this book.

Seduction with AI

AI can free us from much tedious analysis, particularly anomaly detection, helping to generate the surprise that is the impetus to imagination. As Georg Wittenburg, CEO of automated analytics firm Inspirient, notes: "Some stuff is amazingly simple for algorithms, like anomaly or outlier detection. Our system can say, 'This dataset has fourteen outliers or fourteen anomalies—no more no less—and here is the list.'"[15] AI is also helping with medical anomaly detection, improving the accuracy and doubling the processing speed of CT scans for cancer.[16]

One limitation here is that humans are still vital in setting the frame: defining what counts as an anomaly in relation to a particular mental model. AI can see but can't care; what matters has to be designed into the system, although Wittenburg's algorithm is able to learn what humans find interesting through repeated interaction and focus analysis on these aspects.

If you'd like to sit here, I'll get the machine started on seduction while I go and get a drink.

Ideas with AI

As an aide to imagination, AI can help with mental model development. One type of AI tool is a "mixed initiative" system, where AI provides input to guide and deepen human decision making. This is applied currently in translation and customer services.[17] But we can imagine this being developed to help with rethinking: as we write or map out ideas for a new kind of health-care company, an AI could suggest relevant data, analogies, images, and anecdotes to feed our imagination.

AI can also help us rethink with visual mapping. Bob Goodson, cofounder and president of AI-based visual analytics company NetBase Quid, described to us the development of his idea: "Throughout my education I felt that my knowledge got deeper, but narrower. I wanted an efficient way to be able to look into different domains of knowledge.

I asked different thinkers, 'Can you point me to a map of everything that's known in your field?' They would talk and I started drawing maps. I drew a map of physics, one for chemistry, one for world history. Then a computer scientist saw me doing this and said, 'I think computers could automate this.'"[18]

Goodson went on to develop AI-driven software that can aid human imagination by creating maps of knowledge (see figure 9-6). As such tools continue to develop, they will become increasingly useful supports for rethinking and developing ideas.

Collisions with AI

Rather than directly probing the world, AI can give us the opportunity to probe a simulation: a model more complicated than our own mental model, but more accessible than the actual world. The US Department of Defense uses AI simulations to test out new tactics and strategy. Charles Waters, associate partner and executive program manager at IBM, commented: "AI-supported, immersive training increases the speed at which trainees and soldiers learn and master evolving warfighting techniques and technologies . . . And beyond enhancing our response to warfare, AI and

Figure 9-6 A map of customer needs generated by visual analytics company NetBase Quid

Source: Courtesy of NetBase Quid.

I asked the IT department for a knowledge map of our clients' needs . . .

supporting analytics can assist in the development of new tactics to deploy."[19]

Communicating with AI itself could also become a form of taking our idea to the world to get surprising feedback. Analyst Gwern Branwen described:

> The GPT-3 neural network is so large a model in terms of power and dataset that it exhibits qualitatively different behavior: you do not apply it to a fixed set of tasks which were in the training dataset . . . you interact with it, expressing any task in terms of natural language descriptions, requests, and examples, tweaking the prompt until it "understands" and it meta-learns the new task based on the high-level abstractions it learned from the pretraining. This is a rather different way of using a deep learning model, and it's better to think of it as a new kind of programming, where the prompt is now a "program" which programs GPT-3 to do new things. "Prompt programming" is less like regular programming than it is like coaching a superintelligent cat into learning a new trick.[20]

Interacting with an AI could become something between engaging a conversation partner and probing the world. We might take an early-stage idea and say to an AI: "Here is my plan for a new kind of bank; respond to this outline as though you were a financial analyst" or ". . . as though you were a science fiction writer," getting a result and then adding, "Now make it more exciting," "Now be more critical."

Epidemics with AI

AI can help us to more effectively spread our ideas by visualizing human networks to show how a business really operates, as opposed to what the formal organization chart suggests. For example, BCG worked with the company Humanyze to collect data on how people interacted in its New York office before and after a major office move to identify patterns of social interaction.[21] Interaction data can be used to detect hidden networks or, as in this case, to design spaces that encourage the spread of ideas across an organization.

One of the challenges with the mental models at the core of imagination is that they are hard to communicate to others. AI could also help us communicate abstract mental models more easily by helping us transform them into images or stories. NVIDIA, for example, has developed a tool that turns a human's broad conceptual brushstrokes into photorealistic landscapes (see figure 9-7).[22]

We can imagine a future version of this technology that enables us to quickly sketch a new product or reimagined business. The tool could work with written as well as visual elements. We could input broad brushstrokes for a future company and have an AI fill these out with elements from great stories, historical precedents, analogies, and images—

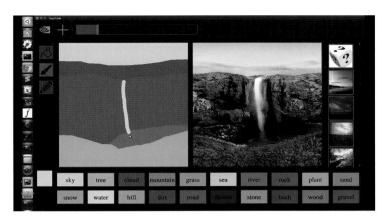

Figure 9-7 AI can turn hand-drawn blobs into evocative scenes
Source: Courtesy of NVIDIA.

something that, with polishing, could help spread the idea and inspire others more effectively.

The New Ordinary with AI

AI can help us extract the common or essential features of successful applications of an idea, which is critical in codifying and routinizing innovation, thus creating new realities. Though AI can't (yet) grasp causes, by identifying patterns it can assist in creating effective manuals, recipes, or user interfaces. Especially as more data is captured digitally on how customers use products, this could bring more predictability to the process of codification. This could apply, for example, in analyzing data from a new method of farming to deter-

mine which features work across different contexts and what is required from farmers to realize this potential. Or looking at usage and outcome data from an experimental type of education technology to narrow down which features to include in a new platform and how to guide people in using them. Importantly, evolvability could become easier with AI, since instructions and user interfaces could be continuously updated based on new digital insights from customer interactions.

Encores with AI

Finally, AI could help us to define and monitor the organizational conditions necessary to sustain mental ambidexterity. Algorithms could, for example, assess the amount of

interaction and experimentation occurring in an organization to help determine whether it is sustaining imagination. Or we could use AI to analyze traits and behaviors of current or prospective employees to help ensure a continuous pipeline of talent for counterfactual thinking.[23]

What Can AI Teach Us?

As well as augmenting our imagination, the effort to generate more imaginative AI might teach us useful lessons about what imagination is and how best to harness it. Regardless of the stage of development of AI, attempts to codify imagination force us to make explicit something that is mostly instinctive and implicit for us. Although humans may be better at imagining, attempts to construct artificial imagination might give us insights into our own imaginative process, individually and collectively.

This could be especially important collectively—at the level of making organizations imaginative. Organizational design until now has been mainly about the coordination of execution. But there is a new, emerging field, called "organizational algorithmics," that treats the organization as an algorithm: a script or sequence of instructions that is implemented in some system.[24] Algorithms don't have to just run on silicon. As we explored in chapter 7, corporate scripts can be run on or enacted by a connected group of brains in a business, which is effectively a network of neural networks. So, the question becomes: Can the algorithms of AI teach us lessons about how to organize humans for collective imagination?

The field is still in its infancy, but there are already a few lessons we might draw.

Imagination through Adversity

One of the most interesting kinds of AI algorithm that has been applied in creative applications is a generative adversarial network (GAN), which works by using two networks pitted against each other, one that creates and the other that criticizes (see the sidebar "Generative Adversarial Networks").

The way a GAN functions relates to a key theme we have explored at individual and social levels: the value of having a multitrack mind and cognitive diversity. What would it be like to enact a GAN at the level of a company? This could involve setting up adversarial networks of people, some which create and others of which criticize those creations; crucially, these should learn from each other as they operate to refine each other's outputs. The human GAN could be enacted via games, competitions, or other ways of creating productive adversity, capturing both the outputs and the lessons to continually adjust each network's way of operating.

Prompts as Programming

One exciting feature of the most powerful current AI algorithms, such as GPT-3, is that the user interaction is based on prompts, not conventional programming. That is, the human creates an input that acts as a seed, generating a

Generative Adversarial Networks

When initially trying to make an imaginative AI, the problem researchers ran into was that when you ask a computer to generate, say, pictures of new faces, it gives the mean of every face it has seen across the dimensions it knows (i.e., pixels), which results only in something that is the average of the distinctive features of individual faces.

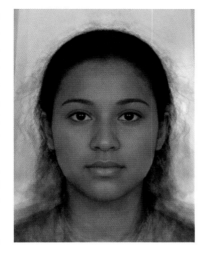

A face created by averaging pictures of faces. *Source:* Lisa DeBruine and Benedict Jones, Face Research Lab London Set, 2017, http://faceresearch.org/demos/average, via Creative Commons.

This is where generative adversarial networks (GANs) come in—the algorithms that created Speedgate and the *Edmond de Belamy* painting. A GAN is made up of two algorithms, each trying to outwit the other. First, there is an algorithm that generates new images using random noise as a starting point, the "generative model." These are fed into a second algorithm, the "discriminative model," that aims to determine whether the image is or is not a human face, based on the database of real human faces it has been trained on. The generator is "rewarded" for making images pass the discriminator's assessment.

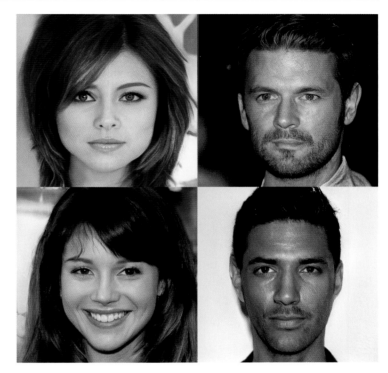

These faces don't belong to any real people. They are not made by combining existing faces, but entirely from scratch. *Source:* Courtesy of NVIDIA.

Over time, the discriminator gets better and better at weeding out images that don't look like human faces. And the generator gets better at making new images, none of which are faces of actual people, but which look convincingly real—enough to fool the discriminator. The two are locked in an arms race, the output of which are faces that are completely made up, but that look so real that they can fool a highly sensitive filter for human faces.

One way to think about a GAN is that it is a basic form of social imagination. As Google AI scientist Blaise Agüera y Arcas says, a GAN is a "a minimal society, a society of two."[a] Two agents—in this case, algorithms—operate together and produce a greater whole. Each agent is trying to minimize its own "loss function"—the function that tells it how close it is to attaining its goal state—but their interaction creates a machine that goes beyond optimizing (creating a perfect average of all faces) to produce instead a diverse set of novel outputs. Agüera y Arcas argues this dynamic applies to real life at every scale, from the cells in our bodies to our minds in society: "It is always a multi-actor story, and every actor is curving the space that every other actor is operating in, dynamically." GANs suggest the essentially social nature of imagination and also the role of different types of minds in creating imaginative outputs.[b]

The notion of competition between different functions is, in fact, supported by developments in brain science. Like GANs, our brains appear to have two competing systems, one to generate and another to inhibit, or question, creations.[c] That

Go on then . . .

Er . . . I'm just recalibrating an inner conflict . . .

conflict is built into how brains work is a plausible theory.[d] For example, an animal might see some food in a dangerous context. Parts of its mind compete, one part driven by hunger, another by fear. Rather than some central executive function that makes an optimal decision, the animal that survives has well-calibrated inner conflict that leads it wisely in different situations.[e]

NOTES

a. Blaise Agüera y Arcas, interview by BCG Henderson Institute, February 10, 2020.

b. Blaise Agüera y Arcas, "Social Intelligence," SlidesLive, December 11, 2019, https://slideslive.com/38922302/social-intelligence.

c. Marcus du Sautoy, *The Creativity Code: How AI Is Learning to Write, Paint and Think* (New York: Harper Collins, 2020), 134.

d. Adi Livnat and Nicholas Pippenger, "An Optimal Brain Can Be Composed of Conflicting Agents," *Proceedings of the National Academy of Sciences of the United States of America* 103 (2006): 3198–3202.

e. Livnat and Pippenger, "An Optimal Brain."

longer response, which in turn can trigger the imagination of the human prompter. With GPT-3, you can also adjust a setting called "best of," meaning the number of final outputs that the AI produces, from which one is selected to display.

We might imagine this kind of code enacted at an organizational level. Like one mind prompting the diversity of knowledge encoded in the AI, a CEO could create a prompt for her entire organization to respond to, in writing, images, or video. These responses could be selected from, perhaps via an AI or intermediate team, and displayed to further stimulate the imagination of decision makers. Crucial to this process would be speed: the idea is not to solicit fully worked-out proposals or highly produced videos, but rather quick responses that are returned to the executive quickly as part of an ongoing conversation.

He wants the last quarter's retail figures . . . but in iambic pentameter and set to music . . .

Controlling the Temperature

Another idea-provoking setting on GPT-3 is the ability to adjust the "temperature" of the responses, meaning the amount of deviation from high-probability responses. When you are asking the AI to work out a math problem or a factual question, the temperature should be low: you don't want to throw any random jumps into the answer. However, when you are looking to augment counterfactual thinking, it makes sense to turn the temperature up.

We can imagine enacting this code at the level of an organization, too. Ideally, the leadership of a business has the ability to adjust the temperature settings for different parts of the organization, or particular workstreams within projects. Some companies do this already, with moonshot departments that work on wilder projects. But we could push this to become a principle that runs throughout an entire company. A manager could request every piece of work with a temperature scale of one to ten. The manager might ask for some analysis of last quarter's retail with a temperature of one ("just get me the facts we always look at"), a temperature of six ("add some speculative discussion"), or a temperature of ten ("ask counterfactual questions and look for new kinds of data to explore these").

• • •

THINKING OF OURSELVES AND AI TOGETHER

While we are far from machines displacing humans, the boundary is certainly changing. It will shift further, and there will be continual opportunities to better understand and harness imagination. To prime ourselves for this opportunity, echoing the words of Agüera y Arcas of Google, we should remember to think of the socio-technical system of ourselves and AI together, rather than of one substituting for the other. That is, we should look for opportunities not only to allocate roles for AI or humans but to enhance the imaginative effectiveness of them in combination.

Chapter Ten

REKINDLING IMAGINATION

You're probably familiar with the defeat of the mobile phone champion Nokia at the hands of Apple. But there's a part of the story that's often left out: Nokia subsequently reimagined itself and became one of the major players in global telecommunications infrastructure. How did it do this and what was the role of leadership in rekindling imagination?

Before Risto Siilasmaa's appointment in 2012 as Nokia's chairman, the culture of Nokia's board and executive team had been conservative and hierarchical: there was little disagreement, "no exploration of alternative scenarios and models," and a "faith that our size would enable us to push through."[1] Siilasmaa aimed to kick-start imagination by getting the board to reflect on how it wanted to operate and creating a set of rules as a result: encouraging disagreement and ensuring every major decision involved the exploration of alternatives—becoming "the informed imagination" of the company. The crisis also gave Siilasmaa scope to abandon the previous mental model of the firm and explore possibilities.

Siilasmaa described this mental shift to us:

In August 2013 we began to focus on mapping out alternatives for Nokia's future. This was difficult, as it was hard to imagine Nokia as anything other than a mobile phone company—even though we have made many kinds of products over our history. But having decided that our best option was to sell our handset business to Microsoft forced us to imagine. It also freed us to imagine: we hadn't explored radical possibilities before because it would have hurt handsets. So we put together a team with the heads of our businesses. Those conversations were crucial—it led to us eventually looking at NSN, our infrastructure joint venture, as the potential future of the whole company.[2]

The rekindling of imagination was successful; Nokia, alongside Ericsson and Huawei, is today a leading global provider of communications infrastructure. (See figure 10-1.)

· · ·

Figure 10-1 A neglected part of the business becomes the new Nokia

Source: Courtesy of Nokia Corporation.

Each chapter in this book has looked at the actions to take to harness imagination effectively. The question remains, though, As a leader, where do you start? What are the key interventions you can make—the fire starters for rekindling imagination?

This final chapter outlines six starting actions you can take as a leader.

Embrace or Precipitate a Crisis

Our initial reaction may be to think of crises as negative events, but a crisis can be a good trigger to incite imagination in your company. Many great businesses were founded or reimagined during crises (see table 10-1). A crisis prompts people to realize that the current guiding mental model is not adequate and continuing as normal is no longer an option; it pushes them to begin rethinking and exploring the space of possibility.

A crisis can be encountered or encouraged. When A. G. Lafley became CEO of Procter & Gamble in 2000, the company was in trouble, but Lafley decided to *deepen* the crisis by doing intensive customer research to find out where its

brands didn't meet customer needs. This ultimately led to a resurgence of the company as it remodeled its portfolio, and organic sales increased 5 percent per annum over the decade.[3]

While Charles Merrill was focusing on Safeway, Merrill Lynch's brokerage business was bought by E. A. Pierce, which became the largest brokerage firm in the United States. Yet by the 1930s, E. A. Pierce was struggling. The impending crisis prompted Winthrop Smith, a leader in the firm, to act. His son Winthrop Smith Jr. explained to us the link between the crisis and the rethinking:

> It was really survival, I would say. My father realized that E. A. Pierce was unlikely to continue to survive as is. So he was going to need a new vision and was going to need new capital, and he basically thought, who better than his friend and former partner Charlie Merrill? That's how it all started. Charlie got really enamored with the idea of returning but realized that if they were going to survive, the firm had to become something very different."[4]

Sometimes a crisis may be looming down the track, and people's mental models need to be fast-forwarded. Nokia faced this problem. Siilasmaa notes, "I don't think anyone on the board had realized that things were this bad . . . Among the board members, there was a 'don't rock the boat' feeling."[5] Nokia's new CEO, Stephen Elop, challenged this complacency with a powerful act of storytelling, taking a

Table 10-1   Many great businesses were founded during crises

	World War I and Spanish flu (1914–1918)	Great Depression (1929–1939)	World War II (1939–1945)	1970s oil crisis (1973–1975)	Dot.com bubble burst and SARS (2000)	Covid-19 (2020–?)
Founded	Boeing	Baxter International	Kia Motors	FedEx	Baidu	?
	BMW	Bridgestone	Dollar General	Microsoft	Atlassian	
	Hertz	Allstate	McDonald's	Home Depot	Pandora	
Reimagined	Rolls-Royce (aerospace engines)	P&G (soap operas)	Dow Chemical (synthetics)	United Aircraft (diversification)	Alibaba (B2B e-commerce)	?
	Renault (tractors)	Merrill Lynch (retail brokerage)	Lockheed (pressurized aircraft)	Toyota/Honda (fuel efficiency)	Amazon (marketplace)	
		GE (appliance financing)				
Invented or developed	Sunlamps	Disney's first animated movie	Computers	Biofuels	iTunes, iPod	?
	Blood banks	Car radio	Jet engines	General purpose processors	Surveillance technology	
	Sanitary pads	Supermarkets	Rockets	Car fuel efficiency	Wikipedia	
	Stainless steel	Ritz Crackers	Penicillin			
	Zippers		Atomic technology			

Source: BCG Henderson Institute analysis. Courtesy of BCG Henderson Institute. All rights reserved.

hackneyed phrase "the burning platform" and painting an evocative picture in an email to employees:

> There is a pertinent story about a man who was working on an oil platform in the North Sea. He woke up one night from a loud explosion, which suddenly set his entire oil platform on fire. In mere moments, he was surrounded by flames. Through the smoke and heat, he barely made his way out of the chaos to the platform's edge. When he looked down over the edge, all he could see were the dark, cold, foreboding Atlantic waters. As the fire approached him, the man had mere seconds to react. He could stand on the platform, and inevitably be consumed by the burning flames. Or, he could plunge 30 meters into the freezing waters. The man was standing upon a "burning platform," and he needed to make a choice. He decided to jump.

Over the past few months, I've heard from our shareholders, operators, developers, suppliers and from you. Today, I'm going to share what I've learned and what I have come to believe. I have learned that we are standing on a burning platform. And, we have more than one explosion—we have multiple points of scorching heat that are fueling a blazing fire around us.[6]

Crises usually impose some kind of constraint, which can provoke imagination. In the case of Nokia, the constraint was that it could no longer rely on its star business, mobile phones. The CEO of business services firm Genpact, Tiger Tyagarajan, points out how constraints produced by the Covid-19 crisis forced people to reimagine: "One day, we got this message: 'Constraint: You can't go to office.' And in five months the entire world switched to working from home—and it's working. How is that possible? Well constraints, or frustrations, drive imagination. People say 'Okay, we're not allowed to do this. Well what could we do?'"[7]

I just thought there has to be another way down . . .

One role of a leader is to look further than others have and bring back what they see to others whose horizons are nearer.[8] Bringing in the bad news or imposing necessary constraints before the world imposes them can kick-start imagination.

Get into the World

Whether or not you are lucky enough to face a crisis, you can often only find the motive for reimagination outside your company. As we have seen, surprise triggers imagination, but surprise is only surprising if it is perceived. Another intervention to spur imagination, then, is to force encounters with the world beyond the company.

Hindustan Unilever, India's largest consumer goods company, provides an example of this. In the 1990s, the firm grew at 40 percent, but this tapered off though the 2000s. We spoke to then CEO Nitin Paranjpe, now COO of Unilever globally, who described the situation: "It was deeply troubling that within months of taking over as CEO, the business was dealing with a very significant challenge—the global financial crisis. We also had a situation where, for six or eight years, the share price had been broadly flat and there was a sense that the business had lost its mojo."[9]

Paranjpe decided to kick-start new thinking. In 2010, he sent all fifteen thousand employees out to meet with customers across the country, to have open, unscripted conversations. On the journey home, they were asked to record their responses to a series of questions (see figure 10-2). Paranjpe said, "Every single person in the company, from me to the receptionist at the front desk—everyone—had to go out and talk to customers, mostly the small mom-and-pop retailers who accounted for a bulk of the business. Everyone was required to come back and share: What did you hear? What surprised you? What confirmed what you knew? And crucially: What new ideas came up? And what should we do about it?"[10]

The effort was not just a one-off: every month, different groups were sent into the field. This generated a number of useful surprises. As Paranjpe noted, "You think you're delivering exceptional product quality and then you find that on the shelf, your packaging is scuffed and the brand name is not visible . . . Or, you shifted from nine dozen to twelve dozen containing outer packs to reduce the packaging cost per unit. But you meet a customer who complains to you that by doing that, the price has become too high and it is a struggle to push it through the wholesale channel." Overall, though, "the most powerful thing that happened was that this changed the organization's capacity to imagine and visualize how it could really make a difference to consumers and customers."[11]

To assess the impact of the initiative, the company measured stock freshness, brand advocacy, customer engagement, and percent of blind product testing wins. All of these metrics improved in the two years following. Sixty percent of the product portfolio underwent some form of innovation in 2012, and the share price grew 34 percent. From being a relatively stagnant company in 2010, in 2012 Hindustan Unilever was the top-ranking consumer goods company in *Forbes*'s list of the world's most innovative firms.[12]

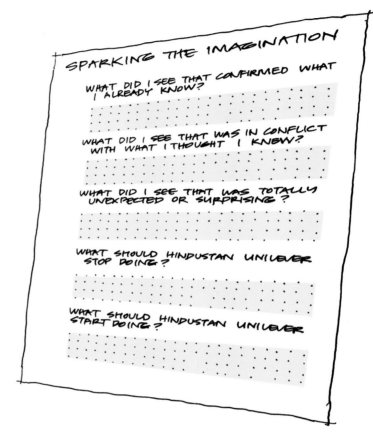

Figure 10-2 The set of questions that every Hindustan Unilever employee took to the field

We're looking for a surprise.

Establish an Ideal

Another way to set your company on a journey to becoming more imaginative is to lay out an ambitious ideal—an aspiration that is inspiring and challenging enough to provoke the imaginations of your employees and customers.

Contrary to popular belief, the ideal can and should evolve over time, as things change and the company needs to be reimagined. Alibaba, for example, believes that everything in the company, including its vision and goals, should evolve.[13] In the late 1990s, its initial goal was to be "an e-commerce company serving China's small exporting companies." As the market changed in the early 2000s—Chinese domestic consumption exploded—the company expanded the scope to "the development of an e-commerce ecosystem in China."

Then, recently, in response to the convergence of physical and digital channels, the company changed its goal again to: "We aim to build the future infrastructure of commerce."[14]

In addition to outlining an ideal, you need to articulate the gap with current reality. The ideal is useless as a trigger for imagination if it simply describes or is seen as blessing the company's current operations. Showing the gap—that your company is *not* able to do this right now—will create the frustration necessary to spur imagination ("Well, then, how *could* things be different?"). And if the content of the ideal is something truly significant that makes people think, "Yes, I truly believe that would be a valuable thing for the world," you have tapped into their aspiration, the other precursor of imagination.

Encourage Reflection

Another starting point as a leader is to encourage people to reflect. Without leadership, an organization's default response in a crisis will be to focus on the here and now. Siilasmaa of Nokia has some advice on this point:

> One of the most important lessons was that whenever you start something important, your first move should be: Stop! Take a mental step back and distill the essence of the issue. Remember the traffic safety lesson you were taught as a child: Stop, look, and listen.

Think of this as the leadership version. And the more serious the challenge, the more necessary this lesson . . . This is not just about stopping to listen to people and looking around to examine the situation before taking action. What I am talking about is climbing a rung higher on the abstraction ladder.[15]

Sometimes, new possibilities can be immediately in front of you, but unnoticed. As Siilasmaa said, "The idea of exiting the core business and rebuilding around the infrastructure business was actually not a leap into the dark—it was a business we already had, we just had to reimagine our mental model around it."[16] Surprise can come from seeing potential in some aspect of the present. As science fiction author William Gibson said, "The future is already here—it's just not very evenly distributed."[17] But you will not see this without the time to step back and reflect.

You need to spread this habit across the company. In the case of Hindustan Unilever, where every employee was sent out to the field, the effect was not just to generate ideas immediately, but to encourage reflection—asking those questions: What should Hindustan Unilever stop doing? What should Hindustan Unilever start doing? One observer reported: "By recognizing the might of employee feedback and encouraging everyone's participation in the innovation process (that had earlier been the domain of the 'brand developers' and 'intellectuals') Hindustan Unilever had opened the floodgates of every employee's imagination and generated a stream of ideas and potential innovations across functions."[18]

I'm immersing myself in a new mental model.

Promote New Types of Heroes

Another starting point for turning your company into an imagination machine is to promote a new type of hero. Established companies offer accolades for those promoted within the core business, those who extract value from the current business model. Imaginative companies must also celebrate those who create new inspirations and possibilities.

When researching the services conglomerate Recruit Holdings, one of the first people we met was Fumihiro Yamaguchi, founder of several new businesses, introduced as "one of the most important and respected people in our firm." It became obvious that Recruit's culture focuses on celebrating entrepreneurial heroes. In our conversations, different employees told us, "people may not have heard of some of our senior managers, but everyone knows the people who created new businesses."

Amorepacific (AP), a South Korean beauty conglomerate, also takes this approach. One example is the origin of its most successful product, a sponge (which AP calls a cushion) that applies sunscreen and makeup together. As a case study reports:

> The initiative, in fact, did not come from the product development department. A young female employee in the sales department first suggested the idea and informally coordinated the development process, which was far beyond the scope of the job assigned to her. Subsequently, numerous R&D and marketing employees and senior executives—including Chairman Kyung-Bae Suh—willingly participated in the process initiated by the young employee. They recalled that although the development of the cushion was not part of their official duty, they all voluntarily contributed their expertise, ideas, and energy to the project simply because of their interest in helping to launch a completely new type of product.[19]

In a speech, the chairman proclaimed: "AP as an organization should serve as the stage where every AP person can build and make the full use of his or her creative capability."[20]

Paradoxically, although imagination is a collective effort, heroizing individual originators of ideas within your company can help encourage others to draw on their imaginations, increasing collective imagination across your firm.

Unleash Bold Moves

Imaginative new possibilities do not come from the mindfully formed; a bias to action is necessary. Tiger Tyagarajan, CEO of Genpact, which was previously part of General Electric, describes the culture at GE in the late 1990s. GE's entrepreneurial culture allowed Genpact to start, grow, and spin off into an independent company: "CEO of GE Capital Services, Gary Wendt, in those days said to me, 'Okay you can try to move this service to India. The telephones don't work there, and you guys want to provide service to the US using telephone lines. It's a really stupid idea, but I'm willing to allow you to spend a million dollars to try it! That's all you have. If you make it successful, great. If you don't, your neck is on the block.'"[21] Wendt allowed others to try bold moves, motivated by a productive bias to action.

In the case of Hindustan Unilever, Nitin Paranjpe's bold move was to dramatically increase distribution. The company was already the leader in India, distributing to 1 million stores and adding 25,000 stores per annum. Growing faster than this seemed difficult. As Paranjpe said, "There were six million stores in the country . . . but the economics of reaching a remote outlet didn't make sense: our sales per outlet were too low."[22]

Nevertheless, Paranjpe set the "ridiculous-sounding" goal of adding 500,000 stores in one year: "We unleashed energy and ingenuity not seen before. The teams geotagged every village in the country and used multiple data sources to identify the opportunities for outlet expansion." The company also solved the cost-per-outlet problem: "Somebody suggested, 'There's only so much we can sell of our own goods. What if we were willing to carry somebody else's goods with us and distribute those? If we find noncompeting companies, they will even pay us a commission and we will make money distributing their goods.' That way, throughput will increase, costs will come down and the whole operation will become viable!"[23]

Paranjpe articulated why the *boldness* of the move is crucial: because it breaks people out of their existing models and forces them to think counterfactually:

> An incremental proposal will be disputed and negotiated within the current way of thinking. If I had gone to the sales director and said we should add 50,000—instead of 500,000—we would not have got anywhere. He or she would have told me, "Well, we only added 20,000 last year," so we would have negotiated it to, say 35,000, which he would have convinced me is a very stretching target.
>
> At 500,000, there was no negotiation. Because 400,000 is as stupid as 500,000 or 300,000. Strange as it might seem, I saw a different energy, collaboration, and ingenuity when the team was chasing this audacious goal. And with that, the same team produced very different results. I reflected a lot on why under normal circumstances people would negotiate down a target—because they're afraid of failing. At 50,000, you would be expected to deliver that number; if you delivered 40,000, you would have failed. But when

you are chasing 500,000, there is no fear of failure; it is replaced by the joy of attempting something that no one had attempted before . . . As a leader, your job is to shift people out of their fear of failure and allow them to experience the joy of doing something pioneering . . . Everyone wants to do heroic things, but safe targets do not even create the possibility of doing anything heroic.[24]

By setting a course into the unknown, imagination becomes our guide, and we discover and do things we could have never imagined in advance of the journey. As brand strategist and filmmaker Joey Reiman observes: "That's what the great writers of the world have always said: that they start out to write one novel, and they end up in a place they never imagined. I wouldn't try to end up in a place that you imagine. I would try to end up in a place *you never imagined*. I think that free will, and that openness and permeability and suppleness on your own part will lead you to a place that, you know, you don't know today."[25]

• • •

Leadership and management tend to be centered on performance maximization, but even high-performing enterprises need to be reimagined to retain vitality in the face of complex and unpredictable challenges. This requires a new discipline of harnessing imagination and new leadership behaviors to support it. We hope that this book provides some first pragmatic steps in this direction.

Notes

Chapter 1

1. Since the 1960s, the proportion of industries in which the top player has led for more than five years has dropped from 77 percent to 44 percent. The graph shows the changing rate at which companies whose total shareholder return is in the top quartile of their industry fade to the mean of their industry. For example, companies that were in the top quartile of their industry in the five years leading to 1990 only dropped around 10 percent back toward the mean in each of the subsequent five years. Whereas companies in the top quartile of their industry in the five years leading to 2010 dropped about 90 percent back toward the mean on average in each of the subsequent five years. We analyzed companies with inflation-adjusted revenue greater than $50 million each year; top and bottom 5 percent of outliers truncated (winsorized) to reduce impact of extreme outliers.

2. Yuval Noah Harari, *Sapiens: A Brief History of Humankind* (New York: Harper, 2011).

3. Carlota Perez, *Technological Revolutions and Financial Capital: The Dynamics of Bubbles and Golden Ages* (Northampton, MA: Edward Elgar Publishing, 2002).

Chapter 2

1. Thomas Suddendorf and Andy Dong, *On the Evolution of Imagination and Design, Oxford Handbook of the Development of Imagination* (New York: Oxford University Press, 2013).

2. K. G. Palepu, T. Khanna, and I. Vargas, "Haier: Taking a Chinese Company Global," Case 9-706-401 (Boston: Harvard Business School, 2006).

3. "A Difference That Makes a Difference: A Conversation with Daniel C. Dennett," *Edge*, November 22, 2017, https://www.edge.org/conversation/daniel_c_dennett-a-difference-that-makes-a-difference.

4. K. J. Friston, "The Free-Energy Principle: A Unified Brain Theory," *Nature Reviews Neuroscience* 11, no. 2 (2010): 127–138.

5. Jørgen Vig Knudstorp, interview by BCG Henderson Institute.

6. Knudstorp, interview by BCG Henderson Institute.

7. Knudstorp, interview by BCG Henderson Institute.

Chapter 3

1. Omar Selim, interview by BCG Henderson Institute, London, May 23, 2018.

2. William J. Freedman, "Neurodynamic Models of Brain in Psychiatry," *Neuropsychopharmocology* 28 (2003): S54–S63 (italics added).

3. M. Moldoveanu, "Managing in the Zone of Oblivion," *Rotman Management Magazine,* January 1, 2011.

4. Roselinde Torres et al., "The Rewards of CEO Reflection," BCG, June 29, 2017, https://www.bcg.com/publications/2017/leadership-talent-people-organization-rewards-ceo-reflection.

5. Selim, interview by BCG Henderson Institute.

6. From personal communications, provided courtesy of Winthrop Smith Jr.

7. Marco Annunziata, "The Great Cognitive Depression," *Forbes*, June 11, 2019, http://www.forbes.com/sites/marcoannunziata/2019/01/11/the-great-cognitive-depression/#34702a5d74c1.

8. Shelby Clark, video interview by BCG Henderson Institute, October 30, 2019.

9. Taylor Dunn, "Anne Wojcicki, CEO of 23andMe, Shares Advice for Entrepreneurs and Overcoming Setbacks," *ABC News*, April 19, 2018, https://abcnews.go.com/Business/anne-wojcicki-ceo-23andme-shares-advice-entrepreneurs-overcoming/story?id=54587273.

10. Anne Wojcicki, interview by BCG Henderson Institute, February 23, 2014.

11. Bill Janeway, interview by BCG Henderson Institute, New York, March 22, 2019.

12. Ronald S. Burt, "Structural Holes and Good Ideas," *American Journal of Sociology* 110, no. 2 (2004): 379.

13. Selim, interview by BCG Henderson Institute.

14. Tim O'Reilly, interview by BCG Henderson Institute, Oakland, CA, August 21, 2019.

15. Katherine Ellen Foley, "Viagra's Famously Surprising Origin Story Is Actually a Pretty Common Way to Find New Drugs," *Quartz,* September 10, 2017, https://qz.com/1070732/viagras-famously-surprising-origin-story-is-actually-a-pretty-common-way-to-find-new-drugs/.

16. "Enid Bissett, Ida Rosenthal, and William Rosenthal: An Uplifting Idea," *Entrepreneur*, October 10, 2008, https://www.entrepreneur.com/article/197610.

17. John Armstrong, video interview by BCG Henderson Institute, October 22, 2019.

18. L. Shulman, "Capitalizing on Anomalies," *BCG Perspective*, 1997.

19. Shulman, "Capitalizing on Anomalies."

20. Clark, interview by BCG Henderson Institute.

21. Janeway, BCG Henderson Institute.

22. "The Web@Work: Boston Consulting Group," *Wall Street Journal*, July 9, 2001, https://www.wsj.com/articles/SB994635999982547003.

23. Janeway, interview by BCG Henderson Institute.

24. Janeway, interview by BCG Henderson Institute.

25. Jane South, interview by BCG Henderson Institute, New York, January 29, 2020.

26. Charlie Rose, "Busy Is the New Stupid," YouTube, January 10, 2019, https://www.youtube.com/watch?v=35sp4S2w9ZI.

Chapter 4

1. E. J. Perkins, *Wall Street to Main Street: Charles Merrill and Middle-Class Investors* (New York: Cambridge University Press, 1999).

2. From personal communications, provided courtesy of Winthrop Smith Jr.

3. Winthrop Smith Jr., video interview by BCG Henderson Institute, September 25, 2020.

4. R. Sobel, *Dangerous Dreamers: The Financial Innovators from Charles Merrill to Michael Milken* (Washington, DC: Beard Books, 2000).

5. K. Friston, "The Free-Energy Principle: A Unified Brain Theory?," *Nature Reviews Neuroscience* 11 (2010), 127–138.

6. Walter J. Freeman, "Neurodynamic Models of Brain in Psychiatry," *Neuropsycopharmacology* 28 (2003), S53–S63.

7. Anil Seth, "Your Brain Hallucinates Your Conscious Reality," TED Talk, April 2017, https://www.ted.com/talks/anil_seth_your_brain_hallucinates_your_conscious_reality/transcript.

8. Seth, "Your Brain Hallucinates Your Conscious Reality."

9. Susan Hakkarainen, video interview by BCG Henderson Institute, December 10, 2019.

10. BCG Henderson Institute, personal correspondence.

11. P. Jones, *Reading Ovid: Stories from the Metamorphoses* (Spain: Cambridge University Press, 2007), 227.

12. John Battelle, interview by BCG Henderson Institute, New York, May 2, 2019.

13. Alain de Botton, email to BCG Henderson Institute.

14. Daniel Gross et al., "Charles Merrill and the Democratization of Stock," *Forbes Greatest Business Stories of All Time* (New York: Wiley, 1996).

15. John Armstrong, video interview by BCG Henderson Institute, October 22, 2019.

16. Quoted in Giovanni Gavetti and Anoop Menon, "Evolution Cum Agency: Toward a Model of Strategic Insight," *Strategy Science* 1, no. 3 (2016): 207–233.

17. Strategyzer website, https://www.strategyzer.com.

18. F. Scott Fitzgerald, "The Crack-Up: A Desolately Frank Document from One for Whom the Salt of Life Has Lost Its Savor," *Esquire*, February 1936, 41.

19. Thomas Aquinas, *Summa Theologica* (1265–1274), "Whether God Exists," Part 1, Question 2, Article 3.

20. M. Tripsas and G. Gavetti, "Capabilities, Cognition, and Inertia: Evidence from Digital Imaging," *Strategic Management Journal* 21 (2000): 1147–1161.

21. The Polaroid Corporation went bankrupt in 2001, and the brand was sold to multiple companies before being acquired in 2017 by a group of private investors led by Wiaczeław Smołokowski, who have brought the brand name back, together with the manufacture of instant film and cameras.

22. Simon Levin, interview by BCG Henderson Institute, New York, March 15, 2019.

23. Levin, interview by BCG Henderson Institute.

Chapter 5

1. LEGO Group's "Developing a Product Leaflet," 1997, https://www.hilarypagetoys.com/Images/articlestock/article875_Image_Lego1.jpg.

2. "LEGO® History: Automatic Binding Bricks," LEGO.com, https://www.lego.com/en-us/lego-history/automatic-binding-bricks-09d1f76589da4cb48f01685e0dd0aa73.

3. Jørgen Vig Knudstorp, interview by BCG Henderson Institute; see also Sara Skakill, "Surprising Discovery about Godtfred Kirk Christiansen Revealed on His 100th Birthday," LEGO (blog), https://lan.lego.com/news/overview/surprising-discovery-about-godtfred-kirk-christiansen-revealed-on-his-100th-birthday-r265/.

4. Shelby Clark, video interview by BCG Henderson Institute, October 30, 2019.

5. "BCG, The First 10 Years Remembered, or How BCG Became a Group," internal presentation, 1974 (unpublished).

6. Nina Alnes Haslie, "Strengthening Innovation in Telenor," UIO Faculty of Social Sciences, August 20, 2018, https://www.sv.uio.no/english/research/applied-knowledge/examples/strengthening-innovation-in-telenor.html?vrtx=tags.

7. Clark, interview by BCG Henderson Institute.

8. Walter Isaacson, "How Steve Jobs' Love of Simplicity Fueled a Design Revolution," *Smithsonian Magazine*, September 2012.

9. "Play-Doh," National Toy Hall of Fame, Strong National Museum of Play, https://www.toyhalloffame.org/toys/play-doh.

10. Liz Gannes, "Ten Years of Google Maps, from Slashdot to Ground Truth," *Vox*, February 8, 2015, https://www.vox.com/2015/2/8/11558788/ten-years-of-google-maps-from-slashdot-to-ground-truth.

11. Chris Woodford, "History of Cars," Explain That Stuff!, March 18, 2020, https://www.explainthatstuff.com/historyofcars.html.

12. Jane South, interview by BCG Henderson Institute, New York, January 29, 2020.

13. "Fascinating Facts You Never Learned in School," WD-40 website, https://www.wd40.com/history/.

14. Steven Ross Pomeroy, "The Key to Science (and Life) Is Being Wrong," *Scientific American*, November 13, 2012, https://blogs.scientificamerican.com/guest-blog/the-key-to-science-and-life-is-being-wrong/.

Chapter 6

1. Takanori Makiguchi, interview by BCG Henderson Institute, Tokyo, August 1, 2019.

2. Makiguchi, interview by BCG Henderson Institute; Recruit Holdings, "Creating Innovation," n.d., https://recruit-holdings.com/sustainability/people-workplace/management/; Recruit Holdings, Annual Report 2019, https://recruit-holdings.com/who/reports/2019/pdf/ar19_annualreport_en.pdf.

3. Reed Stevenson, "This Company Is Japan's Top Contender for Global Internet Domination," Bloomberg, February 17, 2019, https://www.bloomberg.com/news/features/2019-02-17/recruit-is-japan-s-top-contender-for-global-internet-domination.

4. ¥78.9 billion. Recruit Holdings, Annual Report 2019.

5. Eduard Marbach, video interview by BCG Henderson Institute, May 3, 2019.

6. Morclean, "History of the Vacuum Cleaner," n.d., http://www.morclean.co.uk/History%20of%20the%20Vacuum%20Cleaner.

7. Hans-Jörg Schmid, "New Words in the Mind: Concept-Formation and Entrenchment of Neologisms," *Anglia* 126, no. 1 (December 2008): 1–36.

8. *Oxford English Dictionary*, online edition

9. Friedrich Nietzsche, *Daybreak: Thoughts on the Prejudices of Morality*, ed. Maudemarie Clark and Brian Leiter; trans. R. J. Hollingdale (Cambridge, UK: Cambridge University Press, 1997).

10. W. H. Smith, *Catching Lightning in a Bottle: How Merrill Lynch Revolutionized the Financial World* (Hoboken, NJ: Wiley, 2013), 197.

11. Ushma Patel, "Hasson Brings Real Life into the Lab to Examine Cognitive Processing," Princeton University, press release, December 5, 2011, https://www.princeton.edu/main/news/archive/S32/27/76E76/index.xml?section=featured.

12. David Phelan, "'On Monday There Is Nothing': Apple's Jony Ive on Design and Conflicts in Creativity," *Forbes*, November 20, 2018, https://www.forbes.com/sites/davidphelan/2018/11/20/apples-jony-ive-talks-about-the-iphone-design-and-nearly-giving-up/#638517e34117.

13. L. Kahney, *Jony Ive: The Genius behind Apple's Greatest Products* (London: Penguin, 2013), 117–124.

14. "Jony Ive: The Future of Design," Soundcloud, n.d., https://soundcloud.com/user-175082292/jony-ive-the-future-of-design.

15. R. S. Burt, *Brokerage and Closure: An Introduction to Social Capital* (Oxford: Oxford University Press, 2007).

16. Tim O'Reilly, interview by BCG Henderson Institute, Oakland, CA, August 21, 2019.

17. Ronald S. Burt, "Structural Holes and Good Ideas," *American Journal of Sociology* 110, no. 2 (2004): 349.

18. J. Huizinga, *Homo Ludens: A Study of the Play-Element in Culture* (Boston: Beacon Press, 1955).

19. John Battelle, interview by BCG Henderson Institute, New York, May 2, 2019.

20. Battelle, interview by BCG Henderson Institute.

21. Gavin Ardley, "The Role of Play in the Philosophy of Plato," *Philosophy* 42, no. 161 (1967): 226–244.

22. BCG Henderson Institute, survey of businesses in Nordic countries, 2020 (unpublished).

23. Jared Cohen, interview by BCG Henderson Institute, New York, May 16, 2019.

24. John Bunch, interview by BCG Henderson Institute, Las Vegas, NV, August 22, 2019.

25. Anna Winston, "Design Education Is 'Tragic' Says Jonathan Ive," *Dezeen*, November 13, 2014, https://www.dezeen.com/2014/11/13/design-education-tragic-says-jonathan-ive-apple/.

26. Roy Rosin, BCG Henderson Institute, personal communication.

27. Mikael Dolsten, interview by BCG Henderson Institute, New York, May 2, 2019.

28. Dolsten, interview by BCG Henderson Institute.

Chapter 7

1. Commission on Chicago Landmarks, White Castle #16, Landmark Designation Report, City of Chicago, July 7, 2011, https://www.chicago.gov/dam/city/depts/zlup/Historic_Preservation/Publications/White_Castle_Num_16_Report.pdf.

2. "White Castle," Kansapedia, Kansas Historical Society, February 2011, https://www.kshs.org/kansapedia/white-castle/16716.

3. Andrew F. Smith, *Hamburger: A Global History (Edible)* (London: Reaktion Books, 2013).

4. Kate Kelly, "White Castle Hamburgers: The Story," America Comes Alive!, June 15, 2015, https://americacomesalive.com/2015/06/15/white-castle-hamburgers-the-story/.

5. Karl Marx and Friedrich Engels, *The Communist Manifesto*, 1848.

6. Ralf W. Seifert, "Mi Adidas" Customization Initiative," Case IMD-159 (Boston: Harvard Business School, 2002).

7. Rita Kramer, *Maria Montessori: A Biography* (New York: Diversion Books, 1988), 90.

8. Maria Montessori, *The Montessori Method* (New York: Frederick A. Stokes Company, 1912), 261, emphasis added, pronoun changed.

9. "Montessori Helps Children Reach Their Full Potential in Schools All Around the World," National Center for Montessori in the Public Sector, https://www.public-montessori.org/montessori/.

10. Jeff Bezos, 2016 Letter to Shareholders, Amazon, April 17, 2017, https://blog.aboutamazon.com/company-news/2016-letter-to-shareholders.

11. Sam Biddle, "How to Be a Genius: This Is Apple's Secret Employee Training Manual," Gizmodo, August 28, 2012, https://gizmodo.com/how-to-be-a-genius-this-is-apples-secret-employee-trai-5938323; personal communication with Apple store employee, October 4, 2019.

12. Bill Janeway, interview by BCG Henderson Institute, New York, March 22, 2019.

13. Holocracy, "Evolve Your Organization," n.d., https://www.holacracy.org.

14. Martin Reeves, Edzard Wesselink, and Kevin Whitaker, "The End of Bureaucracy, Again?," BCG, July 27, 2020, https://www.bcg.com/publications/2020/changing-business-environment-pushing-end-to-bureaucracy.

15. Isadore Sharp, *Four Seasons* (New York: Penguin Publishing Group, 2009), 96.

16. Phil Charron, "What the Four Seasons Taught Me about Customer Experience," Think Company, April 20, 2016, https://www.thinkcompany.com/2016/04/what-the-four-seasons-taught-me-about-customer-experience/.

17. John Battelle, interview by BCG Henderson Institute, New York, May 2, 2019.

18. Martin Reeves et al., "Taming Complexity," *Harvard Business Review*, January–February 2020.

19. Patty McCord, "How Netflix Reinvented HR," *Harvard Business Review*, January–February 2014.

20. McCord, "How Netflix Reinvented HR."

21. Netflix, "Rule Creep," SlideShare, n.d., https://www.slideshare.net/reed2001/culture-1798664/65-Rule_Creep_Bad_processes_tend.

Chapter 8

1. "Amazon Acquisitions," Microacquire, n.d., https://acquiredby.co/amazon-acquisitions/.

2. Day One Staff, "2016 Letter to Shareholders," Amazon blog, April 17, 2017, https://blog.aboutamazon.com/company-news/2016-letter-to-shareholders.

3. Jeff Bezos, "2018 Letter to Shareholders," Amazon blog, April 11, 2019, https://www.aboutamazon.com/news/company-news/2018-letter-to-shareholders.

4. Charles A. O'Reilly III and Michael L. Tushman, "Organization Ambidexterity: Past, Present and Future," *Academy of Management Perspectives* 27, no. 4 (2013).

5. BCG Henderson Institute, survey of businesses in Nordic countries, 2020 (unpublished).

6. Andre Haddad, video interview by BCG Henderson Institute, May 1, 2019.

7. Jared Cohen, interview by BCG Henderson Institute, New York, May 16, 2019.

8. Magdalena Priefer, email correspondence with BCG Henderson Institute, January 15, 2020.

9. Y. Tsunetsugu, Y. Miyazaki, and H. Sato, "Visual Effects of Interior Design in Actual-Size Living Rooms on Physiological Responses," *Building and Environment* 40, no. 10 (2005): 1341–1346.

10. Ryan Smith et al., "The Hierarchical Basis of Neurovisceral Integration," *Neuroscience & Biobehavioral Reviews* 75 (2017): 274–296.

11. Takanori Makiguchi, interview by BCG Henderson Institute, Tokyo, August 1, 2019.

12. Ed Catmull, "How Pixar Fosters Collective Creativity," *Harvard Business Review*, September 2008.

13. Amazon Jobs, "Leadership Principles," n.d., https://www.amazon.jobs/en/principles.

14. BCG Henderson Institute, personal correspondence, September 28, 2020.

15. John Armstrong, video interview by BCG Henderson Institute, October 22, 2019.

16. "History of the Devil's Advocate," *Unam Sanctam Catholicam*, n.d., http://www.unamsanctamcatholicam.com/history/79-history/351-devil-s-advocate.html.

17. Indra Nooyi, interview by BCG Henderson Institute, April 1, 2014.

18. Martin Reeves, Frida Polli, and Gerardo Guitérrez-López, "Strategy, Games, and the Mind," BCG, March 21, 2018, https://www.bcg.com/publications/2018/strategy-games-mind.aspx.

19. Pamela O. Long, "Trading Zones in Early Modern Europe," *Isis* 106, no. 4 (2015).

20. Ulrich Pidun, Martin Reeves, and Maximillian Schüssler, "Do You Need a Business Ecosystem?," BCG, September 27, 2019, https://www.bcg.com/publications/2019/do-you-need-business-ecosystem.aspx

21. Annabelle Gawer and Michael A. Cusumano, "Industry Platforms and Ecosystem Innovation," *Journal of Product Innovation Management* 31, no. 3 (2014): 417–433.

22. Jeff Bezos, 2018 Letter to Shareholders, Amazon blog, April 11, 2019, https://blog.aboutamazon.com/company-news/2018-letter-to-shareholders.

23. Martin Reeves et al., "Ambidexterity: The Art of Thriving in Complex Environments," BCG, February 13, 2013, https://www.bcg.com/publications/2013/strategy-growth-ambidexterity-art-thriving-complex-environments.aspx.

24. "Dyb.com," *Economist*, September 16, 1999, https://www.economist.com/special/1999/09/16/dybcom.

Chapter 9

1. Blaise Agüera y Arcas, video interview by BCG Henderson Institute February 10, 2020.

2. Mario Klingemann, "The Importance of Being on Twitter," Twitter, July 18, 2020, https://twitter.com/quasimondo/status/1284509525500989445?s=20.

3. Arram Sabeti, "GPT-3: An AI That's Eerily Good at Writing Almost Anything," blog, https://arr.am/2020/07/09/gpt-3-an-ai-thats-eerily-good-at-writing-almost-anything/.

4. "This Is Speedgate," AKQA, n.d., https://playspeedgate.org.

5. James Vincent, "How Three French Students Used Borrowed Code to Put the First AI Portrait in Christie's," Verge, October 23, 2018, https://www

.theverge.com/2018/10/23/18013190/ai-art-portrait-auction-christies-belamy -obvious-robbie-barrat-gans.

6. Courtesy of Wordsmith by Automated Insights.

7. Reuben Yonatan, "15 Ways Companies Use AI to Enhance Their CRMs," Saaslist, May 5, 2018, https://saaslist.com/blog/ai-enhance-crm/.

8. Nicole Martin, "Did a Robot Write This? How AI Is Impacting Journalism," *Forbes*, February 8, 2019, https://www.forbes.com/sites /nicolemartin1/2019/02/08/did-a-robot-write-this-how-ai-is-impacting -journalism/#62b131227795.

9. Deep Knowledge Analytics, "A Breakthrough in Imaginative AI with Experimental Validation to Accelerate Drug discovery," news release, September 2, 2019, https://www.eurekalert.org/pub_releases/2019-09/dka -abi090319.php.

10. David Pereira, "GPT-3: A Brief Introduction," *Towards Data Science*, July 25, 2020, https://towardsdatascience.com/gpt-3-101-a-brief-introduction -5c9d773a2354.

11. Gary Marcus and Ernest Davis, "GTP-3, Bloviator: OpenAI's Language Generator Has No Idea What It's Talking About," *MIT Technology Review*, August 22, 2020, https://www.technologyreview.com/2020/08/22 /1007539/gpt3-openai-language-generator-artificial-intelligence-ai-opinion/.

12. Justin Weinberg, "Philosophers on GPT-3," *Daily Nous*, July 30, 2020, http://dailynous.com/2020/07/30/philosophers-gpt-3/.

13. Agüera y Arcas, interview by BCG Henderson Institute.

14. We have modified Kai-Fu Lee's framework by incorporating the empathizing-systematizing distinction developed by psychologist Simon Baron-Cohen, "Autism: The Empathizing-Systematizing (E-S) Theory," *Annals of the New York Academy of Sciences* 1156 (2009): 68–80.

15. Georg Wittenburg, video interview by BCG Henderson Institute interview, February 23, 2020.

16. Matt Windsor, "Artificial Intelligence Software Improves Accuracy, Doubles Speed in Evaluation CT Scan of Advanced Cancer," *University of Alabama News*, May 29, 2020, https://www.uab.edu/news/health/item /11348-artificial-intelligence-software-improves-accuracy-doubles-speed-in -evaluating-ct-scans-of-advanced-cancer.

17. LILT website, https://lilt.com/translators.

18. Bob Goodson, video interview by BCG Henderson Institute, July 15, 2020.

19. Kevin McCaney, "DoD Gets Serious about AI and Simulation in Wargaming," MeriTalk, February 20, 2018, https://www.meritalk.com/articles /dod-gets-serious-about-ai-and-simulation-in-wargaming/.

20. Gwern Branwen, "GPT-3 Creative Fiction," Gwern.net, n.d., https:// www.gwern.net/GPT-3#prompts-as-programming.

21. "New BCG Office at 10 Hudson Yards Aims to Maximize Casual Collisions," BCG, press release, January 17, 2017, https://www.bcg.com/press /17january2017-new-bcg-office-ny.

22. Isha Salian, "Stroke of Genius: GauGAN Turns Doodles into Stunning, Photorealistic Landscapes," NVIDIA blog, March 18, 2019, https:// blogs.nvidia.com/blog/2019/03/18/gaugan-photorealistic-landscapes-nvidia -research/.

23. Martin Reeves, Gerry Hansell, and Rodolphe Charme di Carlo, "How Vital Companies Think, Act, and Thrive," BCG, February 12, 2018, https:// www.bcg.com/publications/2018/vital-companies-think-act-thrive.aspx.

24. Mihnea Moldoveanu, "Intelligent Artificiality: Why 'AI' Does Not Live Up to Its Hype—and How to Make It More Useful Than It Currently Is," *The European Business Review*, July 26, 2019.

Chapter 10

1. Risto Siilasmaa, video interview by BCG Henderson Institute, June 16, 2020.

2. Siilasmaa, interview by BCG Henderson Institute.

3. Patricia Sellers, "P&G: Teaching an Old Dog New Tricks," *Fortune*, May 31, 2004.

4. Winthrop Smith Jr., video interview by BCG Henderson Institute, September 25, 2020.

5. Risto Siilasmaa, *Transforming NOKIA: The Power of Paranoid Optimism to Lead through Colossal Change* (New York: McGraw-Hill Education, 2019).

6. "Nokia CEO Stephen Elop's 'Burning Platform' Memo," *Wall Street Journal*, February 9, 2011, https://www.wsj.com/articles/BL-TEB-2031.

7. Tiger Tyagarajan, video interview by BCG Henderson Institute, August 10, 2020.

8. Martin Reeves, Kevin Whitaker, and Saumeet Nanda, "Fractal Strategy: Responding to Covid-19 on Multiple Timescales," BCG, July 24, 2020, https://www.bcg.com/publications/2020/responding-to-covid-19-on -multiple-timescales.

9. Nitin Paranjpe, video interview by BCG Henderson Institute, October 21, 2020.

10. Paranjpe, interview by BCG Henderson Institute.

11. Paranjpe, interview by BCG Henderson Institute.

12. Remedios, "Project Bushfire," https://web.archive.org/web
/20171201081839/http://www.mixprize.org/story/project-bushfire-focussing
-might-entire-organization-consumer.

13. Martin Reeves, "Algorithms Can Make Your Organization Self-
Tuning," *Harvard Business Review*, May 2015.

14. Martin Reeves, Ming Zeng, and Amin Venjara, "The Self-Tuning
Enterprise," *Harvard Business Review*, June 2015.

15. Risto Siilasmaa, *Transforming NOKIA*.

17. "The Future Has Arrived," Quote Investigator, https://quote
investigator.com/2012/01/24/future-has-arrived/.

18. Remedios, "Project Bushfire."

19. William P. Barnett, Mooweon Rhee, and Dongyub Shin, "The Rise
of AmorePacific," Case SM 274 (Palo Alto, CA, Stanford Graduate School of
Business, 2017).

20. Barnett et al., "The Rise of AmorePacific."

21. Tyagarajan, interview by BCG Henderson Institute.

22. Paranjpe, interview by BCG Henderson Institute.

23. Paranjpe, interview by BCG Henderson Institute.

24. Paranjpe, interview by BCG Henderson Institute.

25. Joey Reiman, video interview by BCG Henderson Institute, May 7,
2019.

Index

Acknowledgments

The authors would like to thank all the people we interviewed for this book. They are (in alphabetical order): Blaise Agüera y Arcas, Stephen Aizenstat, John Armstrong, John Battelle, John Beddington, Bastian Bergmann, Susan Blackmore, Alain de Botton, John Bunch, Shelby Clark, Philip Clouts, Jared Cohen, Claus Dierksmeier, Mikael Dolsten, Thomas Fink, Tom Friedman, Bob Goodson, Mizue Goyama, Andre Haddad, Susan Hakkarainen, Tony Hsieh, Bill Janeway, Alex Katz, Georg Kell, Jørgen Vig Knudstorp, Tim Leberecht, Kai-Fu Lee, Simon Levin, Jim Loree, Takanori Makiguchi, Eduard Marbach, Antonella Mei-Pochtler, Peder Nielsen, Tim O'Reilly, Olivier Oullier, Nitin Paranjpe, Magdalena Priefer, Joey Reiman, Roy Rosin, Omar Selim, Larry Shulman, Risto Siilasmaa, Winthrop H. Smith Jr., Thea Snow, Jane South, Matt Stack, Carl Stern, Tiger Tyagarajan, Zoé Vayssières, Georg Wittenburg, and Fumihiro Yamaguchi.

In addition, we'd like to thank those who provided inspiration and critical input for this book: Ron Burt, Karl Friston, John Haley, Gary Hamel, Margaret Heffernan, Michael Jacobides, Rita McGrath, Mihnea Moldoveanu, Indra Nooyi, Alex Osterwalder, Judea Pearl, Frida Polli, Michael Tyka, Ben Weber, and Anne Wojcicki.

We'd also like to thank the excellent staff at Harvard Business Review Press, who helped conceive and develop the book, including: Melinda Merino, Kevin Evers, Anne Starr, Julie Devoll, and Jon Shipley.

Finally, we'd like to express our gratitude to the team at the BCG Henderson Institute, who helped with the development of the ideas in this book and the management of the project, including the core team: Ashley Crump, Brigitta Pristyak, Andras Szabadi, Kevin Whitaker, and Amanda Wikman; and others from the wider BHI team: Salman Bham, Tom Deegan, Gerardo Gutiérrez-López, Fabien Hassan, Ask Heje, Julien Legrand, Ania Levina, Hen Lotan, Saumeet Nanda, Lin Wai Hung, and Edzard Wesselink. Finally, we'd like to thank Mark Fuller, who drew the graphics and created the cartoons that appear throughout the book.

About the Authors

MARTIN REEVES is Chairman of the BCG Henderson Institute, Boston Consulting Group's think tank on business strategy and management. He is also a senior partner in BCG's San Francisco office and has consulted on strategy issues with a range of clients in consumer goods, industrial goods, pharmaceuticals, and financial services in the United States, Japan, and Europe. His research topics include strategies of resilience, corporate vitality and longevity, digital ecosystems, corporate statesmanship, and business imagination. He is a two-time TED speaker, author of *Your Strategy Needs a Strategy*, and is widely published in *Harvard Business Review*, *MIT Sloan Management Review*, and *Fortune*, among others. You can reach him via email at bhi@bcg.com or on Twitter @MartinKReeves.

JACK FULLER is the founder of Casati Health, a company reimagining mental and physical health care. He holds a doctorate in theology from the University of Oxford, where he studied on a Rhodes Scholarship, and a degree in neuroscience from the University of Melbourne, where he contributed to research published in *Human Brain Mapping* and *Brain, Behavior and Evolution*. Previously he was a special project manager at BCG in New York and a member of the BCG Henderson Institute, where he published on topics including imagination, goals, purpose, strategy games, and transformation. As a consultant at BCG, Fuller worked with clients on brand strategy, customer journey mapping, and innovation in products and services. You can reach him at jackmfuller.com or on Twitter @jackmfuller.